Language Teacher Recognition

NEW PERSPECTIVES ON LANGUAGE AND EDUCATION
Founding Editor: Viv Edwards, *University of Reading, UK*
Series Editors: Phan Le Ha, *University of Hawaii at Manoa, USA* and Joel Windle, *Monash University, Australia.*

Two decades of research and development in language and literacy education have yielded a broad, multidisciplinary focus. Yet education systems face constant economic and technological change, with attendant issues of identity and power, community and culture. This series will feature critical and interpretive, disciplinary and multidisciplinary perspectives on teaching and learning, language and literacy in new times.

All books in this series are externally peer-reviewed.

Full details of all the books in this series and of all our other publications can be found on http://www.multilingual-matters.com, or by writing to Multilingual Matters, St Nicholas House, 31-34 High Street, Bristol BS1 2AW, UK.

NEW PERSPECTIVES ON LANGUAGE AND EDUCATION: 80

Language Teacher Recognition

Narratives of Filipino English Teachers in Japan

Alison Stewart

MULTILINGUAL MATTERS
Bristol • Jackson

https://doi.org/10.21832/STEWAR7895
Library of Congress Cataloging in Publication Data
A catalog record for this book is available from the Library of Congress.
Names: Stewart, Alison - author.
Title: Language Teacher Recognition: Narratives of Filipino English Teachers in
  Japan/Alison Stewart.
Description: Bristol; Blue Ridge Summit: Multilingual Matters, [2020] | Series:
  New Perspectives on Language and Education: 80 | Includes bibliographical
  references and indexes. | Summary: "This book presents the career narratives of
  an under-researched group of teachers: immigrant Filipino teachers of English
  working mainly with young and very young learners in Japan. It provides a
  nuanced and revealing critique of poststructuralist views of identity and proposes
  recognition theories as an alternative perspective"—Provided by publisher.
Identifiers: LCCN 2019047147 (print) | LCCN 2019047148 (ebook) | ISBN
  9781788927895 (hardback) | ISBN 9781788927901 (pdf) | ISBN 9781788927918
  (epub) | ISBN 9781788927925 (kindle edition)
Subjects: LCSH: Filipino English Teacher in Japan (Professional association) |
  English teachers—Japan—Attitudes. | English teachers—Psychology. | English
  language—Study and teaching (Elementary)—Japan. | Filipinos—Japan—Attitudes.
  | Filipinos—Japan—Social conditions. | Foreign workers—Japan—Attitudes. |
  Recognition (Philosophy) | Identity (Philosophical concept)—Social aspects—Japan.
Classification: LCC PE1068.J3 S74 2020 (print) | LCC PE1068.J3 (ebook) |
  DDC 428.0071/052—dc23 LC record available at https://lccn.loc.gov/2019047147
LC ebook record available at https://lccn.loc.gov/2019047148

British Library Cataloguing in Publication Data
A catalogue entry for this book is available from the British Library.

ISBN-13: 978-1-78892-789-5 (hbk)
ISBN-13: 978-1-83668-149-6 (pbk)

Multilingual Matters
UK: St Nicholas House, 31-34 High Street, Bristol BS1 2AW, UK.
USA: Ingram, Jackson, TN, USA.
Authorised Representative: Easy Access System Europe – Mustamäe tee 50, 10621
Tallinn, Estonia gpsr.requests@easproject.com.

Website: www.multilingual-matters.com
Bluesky: https://bsky.app/profile/multi-ling-mat.bsky.social
Twitter: Multi_Ling_Mat
Facebook: https://www.facebook.com/multilingualmatters
Blog: www.channelviewpublications.wordpress.com

The policy of Multilingual Matters/Channel View Publications is to use papers
that are natural, renewable and recyclable products, made from wood grown in
sustainable forests. In the manufacturing process of our books, and to further
support our policy, preference is given to printers that have FSC and PEFC Chain
of Custody certification. The FSC and/or PEFC logos will appear on those books
where full certification has been granted to the printer concerned.

Typeset by Deanta Global Publishing Services, Chennai, India.

Contents

Acknowledgements   vii

Abbreviations   viii

Notes   ix

Introduction   1
   Filipino English Teacher in Japan   1
   Teacher Identity and Identity Politics   2
   Recognition, Prejudice and Pride   4
   Outline of This Book   6

1 Researching Language Teacher Identity   9
   Post-structuralism and Misrecognition   12
   Recognition Theories   16
   The Politics of Narrative Research   20
   My Story   26

2 The Changing Japanese Context   30
   Aurora's Story   30
   Filipinos in Japan   33
   English Language Education in Japan   36
   Language Teacher Ideologies   39

3 Investment and Recognition   43
   Lori's Story   44
   Elma's Story   47
   Investment   51
   Recognition   55

4 Language Teacher Group Identity   59
   Sampaguita's Story   60
   FETJ's Identity Formation   65
   Language Teacher Associations   67
   Recognition: Logos and Awards   71

5 Careers, Work, Morality 73
    Anna Marie's Story 74
    Shin's Story 78
    Katrina's Story 83
    Is ELT a Career? 88
    Market, Social and Moral Spheres of Work 91
    Morality, Advocacy and Recognition 92

6 Different Perspectives 96
    Renata's Story 96
    Carmela's Story 101
    Self-Categorisation Analysis 108
    Analysis of Personal Pronoun Use 109
    Outsiders' Representation of FETJ 110

7 Conclusions 113
    Identity Politics: Widening the Research Horizon 114
    Identity Metaphors: Problematising Concepts 117
    Teacher Communities: Mutual Recognition 119
    Beyond Narratives 121

Epilogue 123

References 125

Index 136

Acknowledgements

This book has existed for a long time as an idea, but it took a sabbatical year from 2017 to 2018 to turn these vague thoughts and intentions into a thesis. I am truly grateful to my colleagues in the Department of English Language and Cultures and to the wider Faculty of Humanities at Gakushuin University, Tokyo, for granting me the time and the funding to make this possible. Likewise, I am grateful to Amos Paran, John O'Regan, John Gray and Lesley Gourlay at University College London Institute of Education for their practical support and kindness during that year.

David Block was my doctoral supervisor and has continued to be a guiding influence and an inspiration over the past two decades for his pioneering work on language in society. In particular, I am indebted to David, firstly for introducing the applied linguistics field to Nancy Fraser, which led me to read the work of other recognition theorists and to find a compelling new perspective from which to understand identity, and secondly for being a critical and hugely helpful reader of an early draft of this book.

I am also extremely grateful to the two anonymous reviewers of the book and to the suggestions they made that helped me to clarify and expand my arguments. Finally, Anna Roderick and her team at Multilingual Matters has provided excellent professional support throughout the process from the initial proposal to final publication.

My greatest thanks of all go to the Filipino teachers: Aurora Dobashi, Lori Ligon, Elma Cruz, Sampaguita Salazar, Anna Marie Togasaki, Shinichi Hirata, Katrina Harada and the two anonymous narrators, Renata and Carmela. I have built an academic argument around their stories, but I would like to acknowledge how much their passion and energy moved and inspired me personally.

Finally, I could not have written this book without the love and support of my husband Anthony Martin, my sister Kate Stewart and my children, Ben and Polly Martin. This book is dedicated to them.

Abbreviations

ALT	assistant language teacher
BoE	board of education
CHOBET	Community and Home-based English Teachers
CIR	coordinator for international relations
CLT	communicative language teaching
ETJ	English Teachers in Japan
FETJ	Filipino English Teacher in Japan
JACET	Japan Association of College English Teachers
JALT	Japan Association for Language Teaching
JET	Japan English teaching
LTA	Language Teacher Association
MEXT	Ministry of Education, Culture, Sport and Technology
NEST	native English-speaking teachers
NNEST	non-native English-speaking teachers

Notes

(1) A number of terms, e.g. Filipino, Filipina and Pinoy, are in common use to refer to people from the Philippines. I have chosen to use Filipino throughout this book, except where an alternative term appears in the narratives or quotations of others.

(2) The name of the organisation that is described in this book appears as Filipino English Teacher in Japan Global on its website and as Filipino English Teachers in Japan Global on its logo. For consistency and simplicity, I refer to it throughout the book as Filipino English Teacher in Japan (FETJ).

(3) The names of the teachers who belong to FETJ have not been changed with the permission of the narrators. Two teachers who are not members of FETJ and whose stories appear in Chapter 6 have been anonymised, as have other identifying names in their narratives. I discuss the implications of these methodological choices in Chapter 1.

Introduction

Filipino English Teacher in Japan

In 2000, Aurora Dobashi, an English teacher originally from the Philippines, started a group to support fellow Filipinos who were interested in professional development as English teachers, or who wanted to break into the occupation of English language teaching in Japan. Up until that time, relatively few Filipinos were employed as English teachers in Japan. In the public sector, a government programme recruited foreigners from various countries around the world to work as assistant language teachers (ALTs) in secondary school English classes, but not from the Philippines. Similarly, in the private sector, the large English conversation (*eikaiwa*) schools sought to recruit 'native speakers' of English, which generally did not include Filipinos. By 2010, the group, which came to be known as Filipino English Teacher in Japan (FETJ), had over 500 names on their mailing list with about 300 active members in local chapters that had formed across the island of Honshu. Over the next seven years, the number of chapters expanded further, reaching 24 in 2018, including two in the Philippines, as opportunities opened up for Filipinos to work as ALTs and many Filipinos sought to establish private English conversation schools and home businesses, particularly for young learners. Where once Filipinos were denied teaching jobs because of their nationality, they are now moving into the field of English teaching in Japan in substantial numbers.

The stories that Filipino teachers living in Japan tell about their English teaching careers in light of these changing fortunes provide a lens through which to examine what identity means to these teachers and what it means to us as researchers of language teacher identity. In showcasing the stories of Filipino English teachers, I wish to highlight how political-economic conditions and the ideologies that help perpetuate them are experienced and felt by people from a relatively poor country living and working in a relatively affluent one. And I want to argue that their collective endeavour in forming and developing a language teacher association, Filipino Teachers in Japan, can be seen as a form of *identity politics*.

1

Teacher Identity and Identity Politics

In recent years, language teacher identity has attracted considerable attention with special issues in two major international journals (De Costa & Norton, 2017; Varghese *et al.*, 2016), two anthologies of research (Cheung *et al.*, 2015), reflections by leading researchers in the field (Barkhuizen, 2016a), a monograph (Kramsch & Zhang, 2018) and numerous journal articles and theses. This large and expanding body of work encapsulates a range of perspectives on language teacher identity: cognitive, social, emotional, ideological and historical (Barkhuizen, 2016b: 4). Researchers grapple with a host of theoretical and methodological dilemmas: How should we conceptualise identity and how should we go about researching it? My somewhat ambitious aim in this book is to consider these questions from the perspective of *recognition theories*, a perspective that differs significantly from the post-structuralist orientation that is widely accepted in current identity research, and which highlights more clearly the political and moral core of language teacher identity, as I hope to show in the stories of Filipino teachers in Japan.

I start from the very basic proposition that identity matters. It matters to us psychologically as the basis of our sense of self-respect and ontological security (Giddens, 1991; Honneth, 1995, 2012; Ricoeur, 2005; Taylor, 1989, 1994), and it matters when our knowledge and skills are not recognised by others as respectable members of society, when we are denied the chance to do valuable work or be rewarded accordingly. The struggle for recognition features prominently in the work of a diverse group of social theorists, all of whom are concerned with the centrality of issues of identity in the modern world. In differing ways, these thinkers start from an assumption that a struggle for recognition is at the basis of human subjectivity and agency. This view of identity, however, is at odds with post-structuralist theory which has come to dominate identity research in applied linguistics. My contention is that a wider and deeper consideration of the various ideas put forward by recognition theorists, in particular by the German social theorist Axel Honneth, can offer additional insights for our understanding of language teacher identity.

Half a century after the civil rights movements that demanded more socially just and equal societies in many parts of the world, identity politics is back in the spotlight. This is not to claim that the civil rights movements of the 1960s were wholly successful in ushering in equal opportunities regardless of race or gender or other identity inscriptions. But in Western Europe, North America and in Japan too, there has been a gradual expansion of rights accorded to people belonging to social groups who were once seen as inferior or not recognised at all. At the same time, compared to half a century ago, societies in an era of globalisation are increasingly diverse and increasingly unequal. Japan, the country that has been my home for the past 25 years, is relatively homogeneous compared to other affluent countries, although this homogeneity is often exaggerated in public perception (Maher & Yashiro, 1995). Even so, it is a far more multicultural and multilingual country than it was when I arrived, as I hope to show both in an historical account of the changes in Japanese society and through the career narratives around which each chapter is structured. The role of language teaching and of language teachers in this changing context has been and continues to be hotly debated in the media and other public forums. Largely, this concerns compulsory English education, which is expected to lead to the formation of citizens who will help Japan thrive in today's world. Yet, a significant proportion of English teaching does not take place in formal education contexts but rather in a vast private sector of small and not so small businesses: from *eikaiwa* schools to classes run in community centres to lessons taught in cafes or in homes. It is only recently that Filipinos have started to move in large numbers from this private informal sector of English education into public schools. As the stories will show, this shift has been helped by the work of individuals and groups, such as FETJ.

Although my emphasis on theories of recognition is intended to bring a fresh perspective to the notion of language teacher identity, a number of researchers have dealt explicitly with identity politics. An early influence on my thinking was the work of Bonny Norton (2001, 2013; Norton Peirce, 1995), whose ethnography of immigrant women in Canada showed that language learning and social integration are bound up with issues of identity, such as gender and social class. Focusing my research on the identity of English language teachers, I have been inspired by the groundbreaking work on social justice issues involving race, gender and class by applied linguists such as Ros Appleby, David Block, Ryuko Kubota, Angel Lin, Bill Johnston, Brian Morgan, Suhanthie Motha, Diane Nagatomo and Stephanie Vandrick, to name but a few. I have also been keenly interested in the politics of English following a critical rethinking that has emerged on the status and role of English in the world.

From my first encounter with FETJ in 2010, I realised that identity was a salient issue for the group and for its members. Here was a case of identity politics in action. The group that calls itself Filipino English Teacher in Japan trains and supports Filipinos (and others) to become successful teachers. Individually, successful teachers take pride in their achievements and the recognition they attract for those achievements; as a group, FETJ celebrates Filipino identity and seeks to instil pride in its members as Filipinos and to improve their position in Japanese society. FETJ establishes and maintains norms and standards of teaching practice for its members, and these practices are in turn influenced by other groups with similar aims. As a collective, it is a political as much as it is a professional enterprise, asserting a distinctive identity and claiming the right to recognition for its members as potential teachers of English.

As we shall see in the stories that follow, it is evident that identity matters most when individual teachers and would-be teachers face rejection because of who they are, not because of how they teach.

Recognition, Prejudice and Pride

Let me begin by introducing the central concept of recognition on which this book is based. Recognition is at the heart of all theories of identity, and one of the main claims that I want to make is that what is meant by recognition differs significantly between those who take a post-structuralist perspective, currently the mainstream of work on identity in applied linguistics, and a recognition or identity politics perspective. However, the term *recognition* itself is notable for the various meanings that it comprises, a curious and irreducible polysemy that is examined in detail by the philosopher Paul Ricoeur (2005). The *Grand Robert French Dictionary*, which Ricoeur consulted, lists 23 meanings for the French word *reconnaître*, ranging from 'to bring to mind again something or someone that one knows' and 'to know someone or something that one has never seen before by some sign, or mark, or indication' (6) through to 'have appreciation for, to bear witness to one's gratitude' (8). In English, this final sense does not appear in the verb *to recognise*, but it does in the noun form, as in expressions such as 'in recognition of her services to education'. Ricoeur goes on to extrapolate from these definitions a trajectory, or 'course of recognition' from (1) recognition as identification, or recognising other things in the world; to (2) recognising oneself in the world; to (3) mutual recognition, in other words, being recognised as the object of another's recognition. Ricoeur summarises this as follows:

> To recognise as an act expresses a pretension, a claim, to exercise an intellectual mastery over this field of meanings, of signifying assertions. At the opposite end of this trajectory, the demand for recognition expresses an expectation that can be satisfied only by mutual recognition, where this mutual recognition either remains an unfulfilled dream or requires procedures and institutions that elevate recognition to the political plane. (Ricoeur, 2005: 19)

Recognition is an act of power, and recognising others as they wish to be recognised means submitting to their power or their right to be recognised in this way. Lack of recognition or misrecognition is the basis of identity politics, as I go on to discuss in more detail in the following chapters. Recognition and misrecognition are associated with two emotions in particular: *prejudice* and *pride*, both of which have been the focus of some recent research and which serve as the primary analytic tools for my reading of the narratives in this book.

In identity politics generally, pride has come to represent the opposite of prejudice. 'Gay Pride', and the 'Black Pride' movement that preceded it, evoke a celebration of difference from dominant heteronormative sexuality or white Anglo-Saxon cultural heritage. *Pride* is a self-affirming emotion. Its most common meanings, according to the Merriam-Webster online dictionary, include 'delight or elation arising from an act, possession, or relationship' and also 'a reasonable or justifiable self-respect'. In addition to a feeling of celebration (delight or elation), pride is also something we believe is merited. To be reasonable and justifiable, we implicitly assume that others will respect us in the same way. The politics of recognition calls for respect in the form of rights – the right to be different and the right to equality in society and in the home. *Prejudice* by contrast is defined by Merriam-Webster as a 'preconceived judgement', 'an adverse opinion or leaning formed without just grounds or before sufficient knowledge'. Prejudice is irrational and it is hostile, 'directed against an individual, a group, a race, or their supposed characteristics'. What the dictionary does not tell us is how prejudice is felt by people who are the object of such attitudes. But this is the crux of identity, as I shall argue, and it matters particularly in diverse societies, in other words, these days almost everywhere.

Prejudice is an issue of fundamental concern in applied linguistics and sociolinguistics. While different varieties of a language – dialects and accents – are viewed as linguistically equal by sociolinguists, this is not how they are judged in society. As Rosina Lippi-Green (1997) writes:

> Accent serves as the first point of gatekeeping because we are forbidden, by law and social custom, and perhaps by a prevailing sense of what is morally and ethically right, from using race, ethnicity, homeland or economics more directly. We have no such compunctions about language, thus, accent becomes a litmus test for exclusion, and excuse to turn away, to refuse to recognize the other. (Lippi-Green, 1997: 64)

Prejudice towards language and language varieties and the people who use them has been expressed in the form of various 'isms': notably *linguicism*, which refers to the promotion of English and native English speakers at the expense of other languages (Skutnabb-Kangas & Phillipson, 1989; Phillipson, 1992) and *native-speakerism*, 'a pervasive ideology within ELT, characterized by the belief that "native-speaker" teachers represent a "Western culture" from which spring the ideals both of the English language and of English language teaching methodology' (Holliday, 2006: 385). Such prejudicial ideologies, which Holliday (2005, 2018) also defines as 'neo-racist', have a wide-ranging impact on English language teachers, particularly those who are deemed to be 'non-native', as I shall discuss in Chapter 1.

While prejudice has been widely researched, the opposite trope of pride has not received much attention, but it is not without precedent in applied linguistics. 'Pride and Profit' is the subtitle of Alexandre Duchêne and Monica Heller's (2012) book, an anthology of work by researchers who position themselves in a field of 'language in late capitalism' and who investigate the ways that language has come to be regarded as an economic commodity (profit) rather than merely a cultural inheritance associated with the nation-states (pride). Heller and Duchêne (2012: 3) argue that these two discourses have come to be intertwined in complex ways that suggest that 'something new is happening, something that shifts the terms on which social difference is made and on which the relations of power are constructed'. Emblematic of this new order are 'language workers', employees in the 'tertiary sector' of services, information and symbolic goods. I would argue that English language teachers are notable examples of this type of worker, and as such our lives and careers are intertwined with the changing conditions in which we are living, changes that are at the same time material and ideological, local and global. The notion of pride as cultural inheritance that is deployed by Heller and Duchêne is present in my use of the term, but I also want to expand the concept to encompass the more everyday meanings captured by the dictionary of 'delight or elation arising from an act, possession, or relationship' and 'a reasonable or justifiable self-respect'.

Within the shifting national context of Japan, a context that is shaped by local needs and pressures and global movements of people, things, technologies and ideas, Filipinos are taking advantage of new opportunities to better their lives, as English language teachers. Whereas in the past the English proficiency of educated Filipinos was not recognised in Japan, in recent years it has come to be more accepted, and their value and potential as English teachers has come to be more widely perceived. As we shall see in the stories in this book, identity inscriptions such as nationality, race, language identity, gender and social class can be highly significant to individuals and to groups of people in ways that are detrimental or affirmative. We will encounter instances in these stories where the narrators have faced the prejudice of others in their paths to becoming English teachers because they are Filipino, or because they are Filipino women, or because they are older Filipino women. Discrimination silences its victims. Speaking out is empowering, and speaking about success is positive affirmation for oneself and for others who may be in a similar situation. Individually, successful teachers take pride in their achievements and the recognition they attract; as a group, FETJ celebrates Filipino identity and seeks to instil pride in its members as Filipinos and to improve their position in Japanese society.

Outline of This Book

My intention in this book is to go against the grain of much of the current thinking about language teacher identity. By adopting an identity politics perspective, I am implicitly taking a stand against the social constructivist and anti-essentialist approach that has come to be widely regarded as axiomatic in recent thinking on identity in applied linguistics (e.g. Barkhuizen, 2016b; De Fina, 2011, 2016). Identities are ascribed to us and inscribed in us. There are limits to how and when we can negotiate or reconstruct them, and this can be a source not only of frustration or resentment, but also, maybe, of satisfaction and celebration. I want to argue that the emotions of prejudice and pride are fundamental to identity and can, in some instances and in certain conditions, as in the case of the creation of FETJ, be the trigger for collective action, for social activism that demands recognition and acceptance where it was previously denied.

This book as a whole is intended to form a narrative – the story of the changing fortunes of Filipinos in Japan – and it is structured around narratives, including my own, about what it means, and what it feels like, to be a 'foreign' English teacher in Japan. Each chapter contains a career history that provides a way into a discussion of various issues that relate to language teacher identity.

The first chapter provides an exposition of the theoretical and methodological choices that I have arrived at. This is the story of my intellectual journey in academia and is written in a conventional academic style, but I also provide my career history for which I adopt a more personal style of writing.

The second chapter starts with Aurora's narrative and is followed by an in-depth examination of the changing context – social, educational and ideological – in which all our stories are situated.

This is followed by a chapter which begins with the stories of Lori and Elma, two teachers who, like Aurora, have lived in Japan for many years and who have experienced first-hand instances of prejudice and exclusion because of their nationality (among, perhaps, other identity inscriptions). Their stories serve as a stepping stone into a discussion that compares how identity as recognition differs from identity theories that emphasise self-interest.

The fourth chapter leads on from Sampaguita's story, a former business executive who did much to shape the structure of the rapidly expanding FETJ. Since I believe that this marks an important turning point in the life of the organisation, I closely examine the shift of emphasis in its evolving identity from social activism to professional development. The role of voluntary language teaching associations has only just started to attract research interest, so here I review current research and discuss the relevance of language teacher associations to identity formation and identity politics.

The fifth chapter presents the career narratives of Anna Marie, Shin and Katrina, three younger teachers, all of whom launched their teaching careers through FETJ. Their stories lead me to return to a question raised more than 20 years ago by Bill Johnston (1997) 'Do EFL teachers have careers?' and to consider the moral dimensions of the work of language teachers, both in their paid jobs and in their voluntary activity in FETJ.

The next chapter presents narratives by two teachers, Renata and Carmela, who have had some involvement with FETJ, but who do not identify themselves as members. For this chapter, I employ membership categorisation analysis as a way to explore the social identities with which they do affiliate themselves and to provide illustration for a more critical exploration of identity politics and its relevance to language teacher identity.

The concluding chapter brings me back to some theoretical questions that have been touched on but not fully explored in the book: Firstly, given the criticism I have levelled at the use of financial metaphors in conceptualising identity, what alternative might there be, and do recognition theories change this picture and use of language? And secondly, how are notions of community (in many senses, including 'imagined community') affected by a thinking of identity as recognition? Methodological issues are also reconsidered in the conclusion: there are significant limitations to the approach that I have taken in this book. Hence, I end by acknowledging these and offering some suggestions for future research.

Language teacher identity is both an occupational ascription and self-identification. Its value is relative and is bound up with our other identities. This matters when teachers or would-be teachers are denigrated or ignored because of these other identities, as Filipinos have been in the past in Japan. The stories that are included in this book form a case study of language teacher identity politics in action.

1 Researching Language Teacher Identity

I first met Aurora and other members of Filipino English Teacher in Japan (FETJ) in the summer of 2010 when I attended a presentation at a conference for English teachers in Saitama, a suburban prefecture north of Tokyo. I had been interested in language teacher identity for some time and, although I had become involved in other research areas after finishing a doctorate on the topic (Stewart, 2005), I was intrigued by this group and felt that it raised interesting questions that pulled me back towards this area of research. When I approached the presenters at the end of their talk, I explained my interest and asked if I could find out more about the group and talk to other members. My request was warmly received, and I was invited to the first of many FETJ events that I attended over the next six years. Right from the start, Aurora involved me as an 'advisor' to the group, although I had no experience of teaching English in schools or to young and very young learners, the age groups these teachers primarily aimed to teach. I spoke at their events about how attitudes towards English are changing and predicted that as 'multicompetent' speakers (Cook, 1992, 2008), Filipinos would have an important role to play in Japanese English education. Together with Aurora, I signed certificates and presented them to the participants who had completed FETJ's teacher training courses. In return, I started conducting small-scale studies on identity and about the participants' concerns about teaching in Japan, the findings of which I presented to the FETJ members and at conferences I attended.

A focus and a method for researching identity that culminated in this book occurred to me at an annual national event when three FETJ members performed a dramatic sketch of the lives of fictional – though plausible – Filipino teachers in Japan. Each of the 'lives' followed a similar trajectory from various unhappy experiences of life and work in the Philippines and in Japan to joining FETJ and becoming happy and fulfilled English language teachers. Although the skits were fictional, I was told by Aurora that they were based on true stories and I could see that they resonated strongly with other members of the audience. Thus, starting with Aurora in 2012 and ending with Elma in March 2017, I began the 'stories of success' project, meeting with FETJ members who

Table 1.1 Filipino English teacher narrators

Name	Years in Japan (approx.)	Occupation in Philippines
Aurora	25	TV presenter and university lecturer
Lori	27	Medical student
Elma	35	University lecturer
Sampaguita	13	Multinational (US) company executive
Anna Marie	13	Retail assistant
Shin	Back and forth	IT in multinational supermarket chain
Katrina	3 + 8	University student
Renata*	4 + 6	TV/theatre + university lecturer
Carmela*	23	University lecturer, English teacher

* Pseudonyms.

were identified as great teachers, and recording and transcribing their career histories in long narrative interviews (Atkinson, 1998). I returned the stories to FETJ for the group to use as sources of inspiration for new teachers, just as the dramatic sketches had been for me. I include seven of those stories in this book, as well as two more by Filipino teachers who are not members of FETJ but whose views about that organisation are given to provide a more balanced perspective. Table 1.1 serves as a brief introduction to the nine narrators.

My experiences and observations of the FETJ events and of the stories that people told me resonate with various issues concerning language teacher identity that have been the focus of recent research. The mission statement on the group's website states that it is 'an association of Filipino English teachers in Japan which provides support to its members through trainings, communication, and assistance in job placement'. As Varghese *et al.* (2016) state in their introduction to a *TESOL Quarterly* special issue, language teacher identity research has evolved at least partially from teacher education. Questions regarding what teachers bring with them to the teaching role and how they develop their teaching selves over the course of their careers are clearly relevant in this case where the formation and development of a language teaching identity is a primary goal for both the organisation and the people who join it. But more than the process of becoming a language teacher, what fascinates me about this group and its members is the prominence – indeed the celebration – of identities that are often regarded as subordinate or marginalised in language teaching.

There has been a great deal of critical research and discussion concerning native and non-native speaker identities over the years, and the subordination of non-native English teachers has been roundly condemned as the racist legacy of colonialism (Holliday, 2005, 2006; Kubota & Lin, 2009; Kumaravadivelu, 2014; Motha, 2014). Kumaravadivelu

(2014: 66) laments that more than 25 years of discoursal output on this issue has had little impact on the subordination of non-native teachers and calls on the 'subaltern community' to take a set of collective, coordinated and concerted actions to change the reality of marginalisation and the ideology that underpins it. FETJ can be described as a 'subaltern community', but, more pertinently and more intriguingly, it foregrounds a national Filipino identity in its self-naming. This is a social identity that is subordinated in various ways that are specific to the Japanese context, as I discuss in Chapter 2.

Not all the teachers who join FETJ and participate in their training seminars and other events are Filipino, but most are. National identity is prominent not only in the name of the association, but also in many of its cultural practices. Filipino national identity is manifested in the prayers that open meetings and events and in the singing of the national anthem of the Philippines. FETJ events celebrate Filipino identity through performances of folk dancing in traditional costumes, in the giant platters of chicken *adobo* and *pansit* noodles that are served up at lunchtime and in the mixture of languages – English, Tagalog, Japanese and various regional languages of the Philippines – that are spoken at these events. Even the methods of teaching that are promoted, which draw on the notion of total physical response (Asher, 1996) and include a wide repertoire of communicative games and songs, are claimed to highlight a putative Filipino national character: fun-loving, energetic, child-friendly, reliable and professional – and English speaking (Lorente, 2017).

Similarly, not all the organisers of FETJ or participants in its events are women, but most are. Much of the research and thinking about gender in language teacher identity has highlighted the marginalisation of women in higher education (e.g. Lin *et al.*, 2004; Nagatomo, 2012; Simon-Maeda, 2004, 2011; Vandrick *et al.*, 1994), although recent work by Nagatomo (2012, 2016) shows English language teaching in Japan as a space where foreign wives are able to maintain and develop personal and professional identities in a context where such opportunities are otherwise very limited. In the case of Filipinos, such opportunities have greatly expanded in the past 15 years, but they have been concentrated primarily at the level of pre-school and elementary education, sectors that are highly gendered in Japan, as they are elsewhere. At the FETJ events I attended, I met participants who identified as lesbian, gay, bisexual, transgender (LGBT), and indeed one of the fictional dramas that I watched at the annual event told the story of a transgender Filipino man finding acceptance and a purpose in FETJ.

Identity inscriptions such as race, ethnicity, gender, sexuality and social class are intersectional (Block & Corona, 2016; Crenshaw, 1989, 1991); in other words, the combination of such identities increases the impact of subordination. Block (2014) has highlighted the tendency in applied linguistics to ignore or fail to notice certain identities, particularly social class, a tendency that is captured by the term *erasure*. This is defined by Judith Irvine and Susan Gal (2000) as

> The process in which ideology, in simplifying the sociolinguistic field, renders some persons or activities (or sociolinguistic phenomena) invisible. Facts that are inconsistent with the ideological scheme either go unnoticed or get explained away. So, for example, a social group or a language may be imagined as homogenous, its internal variation disregarded. (Irvine & Gal, 2000: 18)

In discourses of teacher education and professional development, specific or intersectional identities tend to be under erasure. But in the social practices of FETJ, the identities that I have highlighted – Filipino, gender and also, to a lesser extent, sexual – far from being erased, are out there on display. FETJ is a collective that represents and promotes Filipinos, helping them to become teachers of English in Japan and as such it can be said to be a form of social activism or identity politics. Taking this perspective has led me to read a body of theoretical literature that is grouped under the blanket term *recognition theories*. Although comprising some widely diverse positions (e.g. Fraser & Honneth, 2003; and see also McNay, 2008), recognition theories converge on an assumption that there is an ontological basis to identity, and it is on this specific point that I want to argue that it differs significantly from the post-structuralist assumptions that have come to dominate language teacher identity research. In the following section, I attempt to explain this difference in order to clarify the theoretical position that I take in this book.

Post-structuralism and Misrecognition

The concept of language teacher identity has attracted strong and sustained interest among researchers over recent years (e.g. Barkhuizen, 2016a; Cheung *et al.*, 2015; De Costa & Norton, 2017; Varghese *et al.*, 2016), and this proliferation of research has come to encompass an ever-widening range of approaches and perspectives. Barkhuizen (2016b) attempts to represent this variety by constructing a 'composite conceptualisation' from the chapters in his anthology of reflections by prominent researchers in the field. Elsewhere, De Costa and Norton (2017) and The Douglas Fir Group (2015) call for a 'transdisciplinary' approach and propose a framework for understanding teachers and learners that ranges from the cognitive capacities of the individual to the macro level of ideological structures (The Douglas Fir Group, 2015: 25). While this cumulative complexity in theoretical approaches can be useful for bringing new insights to research, I wish to contend that relatively little critical attention has been paid to the more fundamental issues of ontology (reality) and epistemology (knowledge) concerning identity.

In a much-cited article, Varghese *et al.* (2005) advocated a dual perspective on language teacher identity, which they call *identities-in-practice* and *identities-in-discourse*. The first perspective, identities-in-practice, arises out of earlier research on second language acquisition (SLA) and language teacher education, both of which aligned themselves with the field of psychology in which the self is viewed as an essential core of an individual and their capacity for decision-making and action invokes a similar view of identity as a self that endures and develops over time and through experience. Thus, 'who teachers are and what they bring with them, individually and collectively, matters in what and how they teach' (Varghese *et al.*, 2016). Identities-in-discourse, on the other hand, draws on a post-structuralist perspective that views identity as multiple, fluid and dynamic (e.g. Barkhuizen, 2016a; Block, 2007). Varghese *et al.* (2016) maintain that this perspective 'allows us to challenge fixed identities' and, in particular, the 'idealized version of English language teachers as white, middle-class, heterosexual, inner-circle speakers of English'. There are two reasons why I find this dual perspective so intriguing: Firstly, the psychological perspective, identities-in-practice, would appear to be incommensurable with a post-structuralist perspective of identities-in-discourse. This suggests an ontological difficulty: on the one hand, the psychological identities-in-practice implies that language teachers 'have' an identity that they 'bring' with them to their work with students; on the other hand, the post-structuralist identities-in-discourse implies that identities are never fixed and that they acquire their meaning from ideologically imbued language. How can this circle be squared? Is it justifiable to apply two theories that are ontologically and epistemologically opposed?

A major (or at least frequently cited) influence on language teacher identity research is the feminist theorist Chris Weedon (1997, 2004), whose account of post-structuralism is worth examining in some detail in order to clarify the key tenets that are so widely accepted. Acknowledging that post-structuralism is a broad church with a range of diverse and sometimes conflicting theoretical positions within it, Weedon favours those theorists who have focused on power and ideology, in particular Althusser and Foucault. Common to all post-structuralists is the belief in the centrality of language in constituting identity and a basic assumption regarding the 'impossibility of fixing meaning once and for all' (Weedon, 1997: 82). Power is enshrined in and wielded through language, but this means that it can be challenged by deconstructing the language and identifying the vested interests that it contains. Weedon draws on Althusser's notion of *interpellation*, which is elaborated in his influential 1971 essay 'Ideology and Ideological State Apparatuses'. Interpellation is the process by which identities are 'hailed into being' by language, or by 'ideology in general' that is disseminated by state apparatuses such as schools, religion, the family, the law, the political system, trade unions, the media and culture, and backed up by repressive state apparatuses of the police and the armed forces. As Althusser (1971) explains:

> Ideology 'acts' or 'functions' in such a way that it 'recruits' subjects among the individuals (it recruits them all), or 'transforms' the individuals into subjects (it transforms them all) by that very precise operation which I have called interpellation or hailing, and which can be imagined along the lines of the most commonplace everyday police (or other) hailing: 'Hey, you there!' (Althusser, 1971: 162–163)

Weedon (1997: 31) goes on to elaborate that 'this process relies on a structure of recognition by the individual of herself as the subject of ideology which is also a process of misrecognition'. We recognise ourselves in the hailing, but this is not because the recognition corresponds to any reality of who we truly are. The only reality is the language 'which enables us to think, speak and give meaning to the world around us. Meaning and consciousness do not exist outside language' (Weedon, 1997: 31). Accordingly, the process of misrecognition refers to our delusion in thinking that the identity that we have accepted is authentic or something that is essentially 'us'. However, in Weedon's (1997: 31) view, 'we are neither the authors of the ways in which we understand our lives, nor are we unified rational beings'.

A post-structuralist perspective thus rejects 'humanist' (which Weedon also refers to as 'liberal' and as 'Marxist humanist') notions of an essential inner core in people. The more traditional notion of subjectivity 'is used to refer to the conscious and unconscious thoughts and emotions of the individual, her sense of herself and her ways of understanding her relation to the world' (Weedon, 1997: 32). Instead of subjectivity, Weedon advocates the terms 'the subject' and 'subject positions', which better capture the formative and ineluctable influence of ideology on the individual. In this account, discourse is everything and power is everywhere. What makes post-structuralism such a compelling theory in Weedon's (1997: 32) view is that 'the political significance of decentering the subject and abandoning belief in essential subjectivity is that it opens it up to change'. Weedon illustrates this with an example of how many new mothers suffer from feelings of inadequacy. The reason for this suffering is that the new mother finds herself 'inserted in a discourse of motherhood in which she is exposed to childcare demands structured by the social relations of the patriarchal nuclear family' and this contradiction 'may leave her feeling an unnatural or bad parent' (Weedon, 1997: 33). Because she is exposed to conflicting discourses, one in which she is supposed to find fulfilment in motherhood and another in which she is economically and socially dependent on her husband, 'she is *subjected* to their contradictions at great emotional cost' (Weedon, 1997: 33). By sharing experiences with other women in the same situation, the new mother can become aware that her difficulties are created by the system, not by her own failings. Post-structuralist feminism aims to deconstruct the discourse of patriarchal power and advocates that new, alternative discourses be created that are empowering for women.

The key point in Weedon's account of subject formation with which I take issue is her explanation of how individuals misrecognise the ideological nature of the subject positions they adopt, believing that they are the authors of their identities. In Weedon's (1997: 31, my italics) view, 'It is the *imaginary* quality of the individual's identification with a subject position which gives it so much psychological and emotional force', but why should we accept that an imaginary or false self-identification is the root cause of so much strong emotion?

Stuart Hall, another post-structuralist thinker, gives a slightly different account of this process. In Hall's view, identities are formed by a 'temporary attachment to the subject positions which discursive practices construct for us':

> They are the result of a successful articulation or 'chaining' of the subject into the flow of discourse [...]. The notion that an effective suturing of the subject to a subject-position requires not only that the subject is 'hailed', but that the subject invests in the position, means that suturing has to be thought of as an articulation, rather than a one-sided process, and that in turn places identification, if not identities, firmly on the theoretical agenda. (Hall, 1996: 6)

The metaphor of 'suturing' evokes the temporary or contingent quality of subject positions, but it is a somewhat strange image, since stitches in clothes or in skin are usually inserted as a precursor to a more permanent attachment or reattachment. More convincing is Hall's injunction to think of suturing as 'an articulation', signalling the perlocutionary force of language (Austin, 1976). Hall's definition portrays subject-positioning as a two-sided process, in which the individual 'invests' in the position they are hailed into. The notion of 'investment' has had a great deal of purchase in language teacher identity research, bringing to the fore a sense of individual agency. But this enhanced sense of agency glosses over the effects of power (Block, 2013), and fails to explain the constraints that individuals may have in choosing certain subject positions. Indeed, the term *investment* as a metaphor with multiple meanings is something that I would argue is quite problematic in other ways, as I shall elaborate in later chapters.

The problem of subject positions is discussed critically in a recent book by John Gray and Tom Morton (2018). Taking Hall's definition as a starting point, they ask:

> How [...] can identity be said to entail a temporary point of attachment to a subject position (and therefore to some extent be inherently ephemeral) and at the same time be used to discuss more enduring senses of self in terms of gender, race and class? (Gray & Morton, 2018: 14)

One way of answering the question is to posit that engagement in identity politics entails acting *as if* identities were fixed, or *strategic essentialism*, a term coined by the Indian postcolonial literary critic and philosopher Gayatri Spivak. In her famous essay 'Can the Subaltern Speak' (Spivak, 1988), strategic essentialism is used to refer to a political tactic in which minority groups, nationalities or ethnic groups mobilise on the basis of shared gendered, cultural or political identity to represent themselves in order to achieve political aims. As I hope to show in this book, this term resonates strongly with the aims and practices of FETJ, particularly in the first years of the association's existence. Gray and Morton (2018: 25) argue that:

> queer or feminist scholars [...] may hold the view that sexual and gender identities are socially constructed (and therefore culturally contingent) rather than always and everywhere the same across time and space. At the same time they may argue for women's rights and lesbian and gay rights in the present *as if* gendered and sexual identities were more ontologically secure than they believe them to be, and all the while believing in a post-gender, queerer future where such identities might cease to exist. (Gray & Morton, 2018: 25)

Although this example suggests how post-structuralism might be squared with identity politics, it is highly idealistic in imagining a future where gender and sexuality no longer figure as identities. Of course, the point that Gray and Morton are making is that identities that are currently subordinated should be seen as equal. But elimination of identities is not generally seen as the ultimate aim of identity politics: pride movements, for example, assert and celebrate their identities and their difference from the mainstream. Far from extinguishing their identity, the aim in such groups is to strengthen their identity, securing rights that have previously been denied because, as a group, they have been oppressed or ignored.

Another way to address the problem of subject positions is to reconsider the nature of the point of attachment between the individual and the social. Following Althusser, subsequent post-structuralist identity theorists have seen the act of identification as an exercise of power in which the individual is subjected to particular discursive positions. Hall's contention that the subject's 'articulation' of a position invokes agency does not obscure the fact that such positions are always shaped by ideology and, as such, impose restrictions on the individual's own power. An alternative perspective on the point of attachment between the individual and the social is provided by *recognition theories*.

Recognition Theories

Post-structuralism and recognition theories share common origins in the insights afforded by the 18th-century philosophers Fichte and Hegel that identity is 'intersubjective', a premise that contradicts the still influential view of identity that was stated most assertively by Descartes. Descartes' famous dictum '*cogito ergo sum*' denotes a theory of consciousness in which the mind is characterised as a private sphere and introspection as the way to achieve knowledge of the self. This atomistic view of identity thus separates the psychological from the social. In *Foundations of Natural Right*, Johann Fichte (1762–1814) accepted that a person ('I' or ego) must recognise themselves as an individual in order to grasp that they are free. However, in order for such self-recognition to occur, Fichte argued that the individual must recognise themselves as 'summoned' by another individual. In other words, we must acknowledge the claims of other free individuals to understand that we are capable of action and that we are free. Thus, our freedom is made possible by others, but it is at the same time also limited by their claims on us. Similarly, other people can only recognise themselves as free when they are recognised as such. In this way, Fichte demonstrated that freedom and self-understanding are dependent upon mutual recognition. Fichte's theory of intersubjectivity was further developed by G.W.F. Hegel (1770–1831). Most significantly, in his work *Phenomenology of the Spirit*, Hegel introduced the idea that recognition is achieved through 'struggle'. Accordingly, in order to affirm one's own identity and freedom, it is necessary to objectify or negate and hence curtail the freedom of the other. However, we realise that we can only gain true recognition from others who are also free. Paradoxically, autonomy is never simply given or guaranteed, but has to be mediated through our relations with other people; it is through the intersubjective recognition of freedom that rights come to be realised and upheld through social institutions (McQueen, 2015).

Both post-structuralist and recognition theories thus take 'recognition' as the point of connection between the individual and society. However, as I have shown, a post-structuralist view of recognition (interpellation) 'relies on a structure of recognition by the individual of herself as the subject of ideology which is also a process of misrecognition' (Weedon, 1997: 30) and, thus, the individual is always locked into ideological subject positions even though she believes that she is free. By contrast, recognition theories view the self and the other as mutually co-constructed and a desire for recognition or affirmation as the basis of identity and of individual freedom.

As with post-structuralism, recognition theories include thinkers who occupy a range of positions (see McNay, 2008), with one spectrum in the range represented by the opposing positions of the German social theorist Axel Honneth (1995, 2012) on one side and American feminist thinker Nancy Fraser (2000, 2009, 2013) on the other. Honneth (1995) puts forward the strong ontogenetic claim that it is the desire for recognition that constitutes the basic structure of subjectivity and that is realised in the institutions of family, society and the legal system. Lack of recognition, in his view, provides a rationale and impetus for social struggle. Fraser (2000: 112–113), by contrast, takes a more political stance, arguing that this understanding of recognition as social struggle 'displaces economic inequalities from view and reifies oppression as an injury to the self's eternal need for affirmation'. Instead of what she argues is the 'normative monism' of Honneth's vision, Fraser advocates a perspectival dualism, whereby social justice is achieved not only by social recognition but also by economic redistribution.

Recognition theories place an emphasis on the affective or psychic nature of identity, which is missing from the post-structuralist account. This is not to deny the importance of ideology and power. Charles Taylor (1989, 1994), for example, argues that what we think of as our unique and autonomous identity is not a natural state but is in fact a modern phenomenon, shaped by religious, cultural and political movements of the past 500 years. Taylor traces the modern notion of identity to Martin Luther, whose assertion that faith was a moral choice rather than simply a following of convention can be seen as the origin of a radically new sense of self, and consequently of revolutionary new ideas about society. These ideas were explored through the writings of Rousseau who viewed the self as a moral and a political force. The notion of the self as a moral and political agent leads logically to a view that an ethical society must uphold the rights of the individual. But, simultaneously, this logic also led from the French Revolution onward to the assertion of nationalism, the right of people who share a culture and language to self-determination.

The logic of recognition, thus, leads back to the problem of power that is raised by Althusser's concept of interpellation. Challenged over an inadequate account of power in his earlier works, Honneth (2012) addresses the problem of ideology in his book *The I in We*. How are we to explain cases where recognition fails to promote autonomy but instead engenders attitudes that conform to practices of domination? Honneth cites historical examples of the Uncle Tom character who takes 'pride' in his service but who is also a compliant servant in a slave-owning society, the 'good' mother and housewife who finds fulfilment in the domestic sphere though denied full participation in other areas of social life, and the 'heroic' soldier who gives up his life for his country. Isn't the recognition that is given and received in such instances merely an instrument of racist, patriarchal and militaristic ideology? Not necessarily, argues Honneth. It is easier to perceive social domination in hindsight. More importantly, Honneth posits a distinction between ideological recognition, or what is taken for granted in the 'lifeworld', and moral recognition by which the individual or group is recognised for their qualities. It is this moral recognition that we strive for in various spheres of our lives, recognition that is manifested in the form of love, social standing and legal rights. A post-structuralist view, following Althusser, assumes that every form of recognition represents an instance of ideology, and thus the individual is always locked into some form of ideology. In Honneth's (2012: 85) view, however, recognition entails respect for another's worth; it is 'a way of rationally responding to evaluative qualities we have learned to perceive in others to the degree that we have been integrated into the second nature of our lifeworld'. This rationality, hedged though it is by ideology or culture, brings into view an assumption that an individual's qualities are real, and that our recognition of them is also real. Rationality also implies that the individual has some autonomy, since actions such as recognition are based on criteria for which there can be good reasons, and this possibility of freedom opens a space for ideological and social change. This realist perspective is termed by Honneth as a *moderate value realism.*

Recognition theories as an alternative to post-structuralist theories have been considered by Block (2014) in his book *Social Class in Applied Linguistics,* although in the debate between Fraser and Honneth, he has sided with Fraser and her argument that social justice is possible only through intervention in the realm of political economy rather than simply through identity politics. Block has also advocated a critical realist approach to understanding identity, inspired by the work of the philosopher Roy Bhaskar (1998, 2002), that corresponds to some extent with the moderate value realism espoused by Honneth. For Block (2014), critical realism means

> being a realist with regards to ontology (it is intransitive, existing independently of the activity of individuals) and a relativist with regard to epistemology (theoretical work is transitive, in that scientific experience changes, as do conceptions of the studied world). (Block, 2014: 19)

In other words, we live in a real world that is the same for everyone, but the way we understand the world differs across time and space and affiliation. For Block and Bhaskar, this approach leads to an emphasis on social conditions and hence to questions of distribution and social class. The approach that I take in this book is similar: I also assume that the world exists independently of the way we think about it. However, more importantly, I maintain that there exists a psychic or affective reality to identity that is manifested in positive feelings of pride where achievements and qualities are recognised and in negative feelings of hurt or prejudice where they are not. Recognition theories provide ontological grounds for focusing on issues of social justice, and hence provide support for an ethical or moral turn in applied linguistics (De Costa, 2015; Morgan & Clarke, 2011). They also provide ontological grounds for focusing on emotions, particularly those connected with recognition, such as prejudice and pride, and this adds weight to a recent research focus on emotions in identity (Agudo, 2018; Benesch, 2012, 2017; Wolff & De Costa, 2017). As a theoretical basis on which to examine the identity politics of Filipino English teachers in Japan, recognition theories have an obvious relevance.

I now turn to a consideration of the methodology employed in this study, namely the use of narrative.

The Politics of Narrative Research

Starting with Aurora's story in 2012, I conducted long 'career history' interviews with Filipino English teachers in Japan. Including Aurora, seven members of FETJ are included in this book. Two other Filipino teachers who were not regular members of that group have also been included in a final data chapter that offers both alternative perspectives on FETJ, as well as an alternative research methodology. Most of the interviews were conducted in the wings of FETJ events that I attended: in quiet rooms or corners away from the action where I could listen and record without interruption. Afterwards, I transcribed the interviews and 'cleaned' them up by removing my questions or interjections, as well as the speaker's false starts, repetitions and fillers. I wanted the resulting texts to read smoothly as stories while retaining the 'voice' of the speaker. I sent drafts of the texts to the narrators for their approval and made changes where these were requested. Finally, I sent the final 'stories of success' of FETJ members back to the group for them to use as they wished.

These stories are presented in this book and they comprise the subject matter on which I draw to illuminate and discuss various aspects of language teacher identity. As such, I follow a growing number of researchers who have turned to narratives because of the insights they provide on language teachers' lived experiences (e.g. Barkhuizen, 2014, 2016a; Barkhuizen et al., 2014; Kalaja et al., 2008; Kiernan, 2010; Liu & Xu, 2010; Menard-Warwick, 2014; Nagatomo, 2012, 2016; Park, 2006, 2017). As a research approach, however, narrative also presents a number of problems and dilemmas for researchers (Andrews et al., 2013). Aneta Pavlenko (2007) for example, argues against thematic or subject analysis of long narratives because the process of coding obscures the contexts and links between disparate themes. She also argues against treating narratives as straightforward representations of life, as observation notes, transcripts or collections of facts. Instead, she argues, they should be treated as discursive constructions, and as such be subject to analysis that considers their linguistic, rhetorical and interactional properties, as well as the cultural, historic, political and social contexts in which they were produced and that shape both the tellings and the omissions.

The texts that result from the interviews with Filipino teachers have to be regarded in this light as discursive constructions, or more precisely, co-constructions. Baynham (2011: 63) refers to the life story interview as a 'dynamically co-constructed speech genre rather than [...]

a neutral locus for gathering data'. Accordingly, although I omitted my voice from the texts, my role in their production cannot be understated: from my framing of the interview as 'the stories of success project' to the participants' perception of me and various identities that were or became salient in the course of our interaction to the transcription and revision ('cleaning up') of the text. In writing about the stories, I allude to my reactions to the content at the time, and I attempt to situate the narratives in a range of contexts. In doing so, I draw inspiration from a study by Hayes (2010) in which the career history of a single Sri Lankan English teacher is contextualised within the history of civil war between majority Sinhalese and minority Tamils. Barkhuizen (2008) calls this process of contextualisation 'story-Story-STORY', where the initial telling of the narrative is situated within the context of the interaction with the researcher, and that interaction in turn is situated within the wider prevailing social and historical contexts. Nevertheless, my decision to remove my voice from the texts, to turn dialogue into monologue, requires further justification.

In recent years, a distinction has been drawn between a *big-story* and a *small-story* approach (Bamberg, 2007; Georgakopolou, 2007; Phoenix, 2013), where the big-story approach focuses on the content or themes that are contained in the narrative, while the small-story approach attends to 'narrative-in-interaction', that is, how narrative is performed and accomplishes certain tasks, including identity (Phoenix, 2013). Small stories tend to be extracted from lengthier texts of spoken interactional data (e.g. Gray & Morton, 2018), but they can also be drawn from different modes and sources of data. In a longitudinal study of a teacher's imagined identity, for example, Barkhuizen (2016b) takes excerpts from a range of data, including conversations, interviews, written narratives and multimodal digital stories. Viewing identity as multiple, fragmented, context specific and performed in communicative practices, the small-story research is more closely aligned with the post-structuralist paradigm (Georgakopolou, 2015).

The realist approach that I adopt in this book means that I take a different perspective on the truth or ontology of narratives. Rather than treating narratives as merely discourse, I assume that the lived experiences that form the content of life story narratives are real, even though our ways of relating that experience are variable. Thus, if I stub my toe, I feel pain. How I describe that experience or turn it into a story depends on many different factors, both personal and cultural. Thus, with the narratives of the Filipino English teachers, my aim is to foreground the content of the stories, not the form of the narrative or positioning of the narrator, even though I do not deny that the content and form and positioning are interconnected.

Narrative has been described as the primary form by which human experience is made meaningful (Polkinghorne, 1988), and the act of making meaning of our lives (Bruner, 1990). As the philosopher Alasdair MacIntyre (1981) observes:

> It is because we all live out narratives in our lives and because we understand our own lives in terms of the narratives that the form of narrative is appropriate for understanding the actions of others. Stories are lived before they are told. (MacIntyre, 1981: 197)

MacIntyre's point that experience precedes narratives is an important consideration, one that can be lost in a post-structuralist approach to narrative that lays so much emphasis on discourse.

Moving away from the post-structuralist emphasis on discourse also implies turning the focus back on aspects of narratives that have come to be overlooked, including their normative features. In his 1990 book *Acts of Meaning*, Jerome Bruner presents a complex and nuanced definition of narrative: Narratives convey temporal sequentiality, in other words, they (usually) describe one thing happening after another. They are 'indifferent' to truth or fiction; thus, there is no way for you to tell whether a story I tell you really happened or whether I simply made it up – the narrative form either way would be the same. They are a dramatisation of experience, or at least what seems like experience, organised around recognisable plot structures and containing a cast of characters, thereby allowing for a duality in the representation of experience as both external (what is going on in the world) and internal (how the characters perceive and react to it). Narratives are a way of organising experience and, particularly, in managing departures from the canonical. They are thus normative, since their effectiveness relies on adherence to expected lines of logical and moral reasoning, or what Bruner refers to as 'folk psychology'. These characteristics combine to create in narrative form a rhetorical account that aims at 'illocutionary intentions'. Narrative is, in sum, a speech act, a desire to communicate meaning, framed in a larger context of a 'cultural stock of plot lines' in which the normative and the evaluative significance is apparent (MacIntyre, 1981; Ochs & Capps, 2001; Polletta *et al.*, 2011).

The social identity theorist Harvey Sacks (1974) illustrates this normative and evaluative function in his famous example of a narrative by a young child, 'The baby cried. The mommy picked it up'. Although it consists of only two short sentences, Sacks states that this constitutes a 'complete' narrative. As such, it describes a sequence of events that orients the listener to something that is of significance to the narrator (in the case of the young child, the fact that a baby is crying and that therefore something should be done about it), and provides some kind of resolution (the mommy picked it up, and so the problem was solved). Not all narratives provide resolutions, although many do. In their attempt to define what a narrative is, Labov and Waletsky (1967) proposed a temporal structure of subject–orientation–complication–resolution coda, although they clarify that a narrative may be created from just the subject and its orientation. In the 'baby cried' narrative, this orientation becomes more apparent with the resolution 'the mommy picked it up'. But this is an interpretation – we can imagine a child's universe and what might be of significance within it, but we cannot be entirely sure that this is the meaning intended by the young narrator.

As Bruner (1990: 85–86) observes, narratives have 'rhetorical aims or illocutionary intentions that are not merely expository, but rather, partisan'; they work to 'cajole, to deceive, to flatter, to justify'. Bruner's use of the term *illocutionary* refers to Austin's (1976) classic work *How to Do Things With Words*, reminding us that utterances have (or at least are intended to have) a *force*. What this theory of language omits, however, is the fact that force is not so much a property of words (except in the exceptional performatives that Austin cites), as it is of people and groups of people. I can say or write something to achieve some goal, but if no one listens to me, or if no one reads what I write, my words have no force. If I fear that no one will listen to me, or read what I write, or perhaps worse, if I fear that what I say or write will be disparaged or dismissed, I am likely to keep my thoughts to myself. Because words have this potential force to 'do things' in the world, they can be considered instruments of power. But words alone are not powerful: people are. Language is empowering, hence the need for literate societies, and hence the therapeutic benefits of talking (Bruner, 1986). Silence is a form of disenfranchisement, whether because a lack of education denies someone the ability to express themselves effectively, or because some people are not listened to and so remain silent when it is actually in their interests to be heard. Speaking up and being heard bring self-esteem and pride; being silenced is often an effect of prejudice. In choosing narrative as a method of researching and analysing teacher identity, I commit myself to certain theoretical positions regarding epistemology and ontology, as I have already discussed. I assume that the narratives of the Filipino teachers that I recorded are based on 'lived experience' (or at least what can be plausibly understood as lived experience) and that the narrators intend some illocutionary effect (Bamberg & McCabe, 1998; Bruner, 1990) on their listener – me. In other words, they are 'motivated storytellers' (Hermans, 2002).

The choice of narrative as a research method also involves considerations of representation. Despite the prominence of a small-story approach in recent research, I have chosen to present the stories that were told to me in their entirety, and entirely in the voice of the narrator. If one of the purposes of research is to extrapolate theories – in this case about language teacher identity – from data, it could be argued that this is a somewhat messy and long-winded way of going about it. Conventionally, qualitative researchers extract themes, or 'small stories', from the copious amounts of data they have collected using methods that are principled and systematic. Narrative interviews are regarded from an interpretive perspective as 'co-constructions' of meaning (Mischler, 1986) or 'interViews' (Kvale, 1996) between the narrator and the interviewer. However, I take the view that this process is not at all equal. When I listened to and recorded the Filipino teachers' stories, although these stories are affected by my presence and involvement as an active listener, they remain *their* stories. I wish to acknowledge the goodwill shown by the teachers in telling their stories so openly by respecting that ownership and reproducing them as they were told.

This is, of course, a somewhat disingenuous claim: the stories are not – indeed cannot be – reproduced as they were told. Transcription is a practice that is inherently embedded in power (Bucholtz, 2000; Roberts, 1997). The narratives of the Filipino teachers were spoken and digitally audio recorded, an act that already omits a great deal of information. I produced transcripts manually by repeatedly listening to the recordings and I made the decision to 'clean up' the resulting text: omitting repetitions, false starts and some discourse fillers to make it easier to read. I tried to preserve the narrators' 'voice', but I did not make any attempt to represent accent. The stories are presented as 'texts', divided into sentences and paragraphs, rather than in numbered lines of discourse.

The stories are not presented, moreover, in any random sequence, but are ordered chronologically so as to represent a larger narrative of FETJ; in some cases, the narratives do not appear individually but together with others because they provide particularly interesting illustrations of themes that I wish to discuss. Thus, Chapter 3 presents the narratives of two older teachers and these stories help me to discuss the metaphor of investment and to elaborate further on identity as recognition; Chapter 5 includes the stories of three younger teachers that lead into a discussion of the meanings of career and work in language teacher identity; and Chapter 6 presents the complete narratives of two non-members of FETJ on alternative Filipino language teacher identities. These groupings, as with other decisions regarding the presentation of the narratives, are my choice, and as such are political: they serve my purpose in telling the larger story of the FETJ organisation and building a case for taking an alternative conceptualisation of language teacher identity that is based on recognition theories.

Since this book is about identity and identity politics, the issue of naming and anonymity is of singular importance. I have made the decision to disclose the names of the narrators who are members of FETJ. Since this is a story about a particular organisation and since the narrators have prominent roles within it, the convention of anonymity serves little purpose. When I returned the transcripts to the FETJ narrators, I offered to change their names but all of the narrators who appear in this book agreed to the use of their real names. In the case of the two narrators who are not members of FETJ, however, I have, at their request, tried to protect their anonymity by changing their names, as well as the names of people and institutions that appear in their stories. Anonymity is an ethical consideration in research, but it is also a political choice with methodological implications. In the case of the FETJ members, I have refrained from subjecting their narratives to rigorous and systematic analysis, whether in the form of thematic coding or short-story analysis. Instead, I start each chapter with one or more narratives, assuming that these stories 'speak for themselves'. As Vandrick (2009) argues, rather than speaking *for* participants in our research, a more ethical stance is to speak *with*, speak *about* and speak *out for* them. Accordingly, although it could be said that I speak for the narrators by representing them in a one-sided way, my intention is to *speak about* their lives and show how that relates to contemporary discussions about teacher identity and to *speak out for* them as a group of language teachers whose experiences deserve our attention.

Above all, my intention is to tell or – perhaps more accurately – construct a story and, like a literary fiction, to create a context in which the teachers' lives and their collaboration with each other in FETJ are depicted and must be understood. As with literary creations, however, although the book is organised to support my purpose of considering language teacher identity in a new way, it is up to readers, who will bring to the act of reading their own beliefs (Cameron *et al.*, 1992) in order to judge what is meaningful or significant in the narratives. Thus, following Pavlenko (2003, 2007), I acknowledge that the narratives are discursive constructions, in terms of both their initial telling by the narrators and in the choices that I made in shaping their presentation, but I also take the position, following MacIntyre (1981), that they are based on lived experience. In other words, the narratives can be read not only in terms of *how* this experience is represented, but also in terms of *what* experience is presented. In many academic book-length publications, individual chapters can be read independently, but in this book both the temporal structure and the cumulative presentation of teachers' lives entail that it is to be read in the order in which it is written.

As I have tried to make clear throughout this chapter, power and politics are central to the way I am conceptualising identity and narrative. All stories have a moral function (they represent the world as the narrator thinks it should be, and deviations from that status quo are significant) and an illocutionary function (they are intended to produce some kind of effect on the listener or reader). Since I was the first audience of these narratives, I end this chapter with my own narrative, heeding the advice of Park (2017) that 'being a political and reflexive researcher is a must', and guided by the same question that I put to each of the Filipino teachers: How did I become an English teacher?

My Story

Like the Filipinos in this book, I am an English teacher working in Japan. But I come from the United Kingdom, not from the Philippines. Like the majority of the Filipino English teachers I have met, family plays an important part in my career narrative. I came to Japan in 1994 at the age of 32 following my husband who had been appointed to a two-year position as a lecturer in English literature at a university in Tokyo. We had with us our five-month old baby son and during the first year in Japan I stayed at home with him, the first time in my adult life that I had not been in employment or education. During that first year I attempted to learn Japanese, confident at first that my academic background in languages would ensure that I picked it up quickly, but increasingly frustrated by my very slow progress. After six months, a colleague of my husband asked if I would be interested in teaching English, and I jumped at the chance to return to work. Although I had taught English for a language school while I was doing a master's degree, I had no professional qualifications in language teaching and, although I had some language tutoring experience, had never taught in a classroom. But I agreed nonetheless and then quickly found additional work in two other universities which enabled me to qualify for childcare provision at a local nursery for our child.

My first experience of teaching in Japanese classrooms was a shock. I had no guidance from the universities themselves on what to do. Expecting to conduct classes using the communicative language teaching methods that I had learned at the language school I'd worked for in England, I discovered that most of my students did not seem motivated or willing to communicate at all, and my efforts seemed to fall flat week after week. Fortunately, at one of the universities where I taught, I found myself working with a Japanese woman who had studied at the same university where I did my master's degree. She told me that she thought the English language classes were a waste of time when she herself was an undergraduate at that university but had found the classes she took to support her doctoral studies in the UK to be extremely beneficial. She had based her course in Japan on those materials and was finding that the students responded very well to them. I quickly abandoned my original plan, started using different materials, and stopped expecting students to speak to me without prompting. With some classes I felt that what I was doing was working, in others I felt at a loss.

It was during this second year that my husband got tenure at his university and we decided to stay in Japan for another few years at least. Slowly I was beginning to feel more confident as a teacher. But more importantly for my evolving teacher identity, I met a group of dynamic younger teachers who loved talking about teaching. We set up an informal self-development group and met on Saturdays to talk about teaching *and to discuss video recordings that we made of each other's classes. By the following year, my husband was encouraging me to apply to do a further degree in teacher education and I was avidly reading books and journals on TESOL. After giving birth to our daughter, I was accepted by London University's Institute of Education (now University College London Institute of Education) to study on their doctoral programme. Taking the two children with me, I lived with my husband's older sister in Kent for six months and commuted up to London every day to attend lectures and seminars and to study in the library.*

When I returned to Japan, I was immediately appointed to a full-time position on a temporary contract at one university, and then, three years later, to a further contract position at another. Four years after that, having finally completed my doctorate, I was offered the possibility of a tenured position at a private university in central Tokyo, which is where I have worked for the past 11 years. In my current position, I still teach English to undergraduates, but I also teach a lecture course, an undergraduate seminar and a graduate course on applied linguistics. I am no longer 'just' an English language teacher. At the same time, although my current job is one that commands my allegiance far more than any other I have had, my professional life extends far beyond my paid work. I joined the Japan Association for Language Teaching (JALT) when I returned from London in 1999 and have been actively involved in its Learner Development Special Interest Group among other JALT groups since 2005 when I finished my doctorate. There have been numerous times when my JALT work has consumed far more of my time and attention than my 'proper' job. In recent years, I have also become increasingly involved with the international academic community, as a reviewer, editor, researcher, writer, supervisor and examiner, activities which, apart from the last two, are unpaid, but which I do out of a sense of commitment to the academic community. I don't begrudge the time and effort I spend on this, except when I find myself overloaded and overwhelmed; mostly, I feel honoured to be asked to contribute in these ways.

My interest in language teacher identity stems from my doctoral project on English language teachers working in Japanese universities, but identity is something that has puzzled me for considerably longer. My fascination with languages and cultures led me to an undergraduate degree in Russian and French, and subsequently to a master's degree in Russian and East European Studies for which I wrote a thesis on Ukrainian national identity, just at the moment in history when the Soviet Union collapsed. My own national identity bothers me: I sound English (my accent is middle class, some would say posh, not inflected by any region), but my parents were Scottish (my grandfather used to inveigh against the 'Sassenach' English); I was not born in England and throughout most of my early childhood I lived in Singapore, Germany and Australia. When asked, I prefer to say that I am British, but it feels awkward.

In Japan, I have given up hedging or explaining, and simply say I am 'igirisu-jin', just as I have given up explaining that I have kept my own name when my neighbours in Tokyo call me by my husband's name. At the same time, my identity – as a white British citizen, educated at prestigious universities in the UK – has endowed me with social capital that has facilitated access to teaching jobs (as it did to the bank jobs I did for a few years after my first degree). I feel pride in my accomplishments for which I have worked and continue to work hard, but I also realise that my path has been smoothed in my life in ways that are none of my doing.

Living in Japan for so long I no longer feel foreign in the way that I did when I arrived. Japan has changed in this time, and so have I. I feel a sense of belonging to my place of work and to my neighbourhood. But at the same time, I am still a 'gaijin': I look and sound foreign, and this often works to my advantage when people I don't know treat me as an honoured guest. Not all foreigners are accorded such respect and good will, however. I am aware of some degree of prejudice against Filipinos in Japan, particularly among the older generation. Aurora told me of an incident that occurred several years ago when she was walking home at the end of a day's teaching and a middle-aged man in a suit called out to her, leering, 'Ikura?' ('How much?') I've seen it myself, though not expressed so obscenely, in the look of distaste on the face of my friendly neighbour when I told her I was on my way to an event organised by the Filipino teachers. 'Don't they speak English with an accent?', she says. 'Yes, they do', I reply, then add slyly, 'Everyone has an accent. I have an accent'. Of course, it's not actually the accent that she dislikes so much as Filipinos in general. And that makes me, positioned in this way as the 'right kind of English teacher in Japan', feel very uncomfortable indeed.

Mine is a story of privilege and good fortune. Writing about the language teacher identity of Filipinos from this position is a risky venture that has made me hesitate to write this book for quite a long time. What gives me the right to speak about Filipino identity? That I feel compelled to write it now is in part propelled by the rise in the public expression of racist and xenophobic attitudes in Japan, as described in a recent commentary in *The Japan Times* (Russell, 2018), and as seen in many other countries around the world. The identity of language teachers, and the pedagogical role this might serve in the classroom (Morgan, 2004) and in society assumes ever greater importance in these conditions.

In this first chapter, I have sought to provide a rationale for taking a new theoretical perspective to research on teacher identity. My main contention is that a recognition perspective on identity enables us to comprehend more readily the connections between the political and the personal, between teachers' rights to work and their feelings of pride in what they do. I have also sought to justify a somewhat unorthodox approach to narrative in choosing to present whole narratives and in choosing to name some but not all of the narrators. My story, with which I have ended this chapter, serves to illustrate my long-standing interest in identity, as well as to indicate my own position regarding prejudice and pride as a language teacher in Japan. It is time now to turn to the Filipino teachers' narratives.

2 The Changing Japanese Context

The first of the Filipino teacher narratives comes from Aurora, the founder and leading light of Filipino English Teacher in Japan (FETJ). Her story is shorter than the stories of the other teachers in this book: when I started this project, I wanted the focus to be on the teachers' lives in Japan, and so I omitted an anecdote she originally told me within the larger narrative that would shed more light on why she came to Japan. This chapter presents the version that I sent to Aurora and to which she gave her approval. As with all the stories that follow, I will comment on the tropes of prejudice and pride that I see reflected in the narrative. Primarily, however, as a first example of a career history by a Filipino teacher of English in Japan, Aurora's narrative serves as a springboard for exploring the context of English teaching in Japan.

Aurora told me her story in 2012 in a quiet corner of a fast-food cafe in a dormitory suburb north of Tokyo. We were not alone: with us was Cesar, who appears in another of the teachers' stories in Chapter 3 and whose work as a missionary is discussed in Chapter 4. The three of us chatted before we started the interview. Cesar had not heard Aurora's story before and he listened quietly and with interest as Aurora talked, prompted by questions that I asked her about her life and her work.

Aurora's Story

I'm from northern Luzon, where Marcos came from. The local language is Ilocano, but at home we spoke three languages: mostly Ilocano and English. My grandfather spoke wonderful English though he left school to work after sixth grade. People of his generation, their command of English is excellent, not like today where everyone speaks Taglish. English is the medium of education in the Philippines, so I used it all through school. We don't think of English as a foreign language, it's our second language. I don't think we consider ourselves non-native speakers. Am I a native English speaker? That depends on how other people consider me and my English.

I came to Japan 21 years ago. At the time I was teaching speech and communication at the university in Manila. I'd been working as a TV broadcaster and we brought students onto our show, so after that the students said 'Come and teach us'. That's where I got my passion for teaching; that's where it started.

But then I got married and came to Japan with my husband. I spoke no Japanese and for the first year, I stayed home and watched baseball on TV. Then I asked my husband to bring me a newspaper, and I saw the classified ads for English teachers, and I said, 'That's what I'll do'.

I applied for two jobs, the first teaching business English, but my husband said, 'No way'. The second one was for Shogakan teaching elementary school children, and my husband said, 'Right, I'll take you to your schools!' They hired me right away; I was the first non-native teacher there. I worked there first as a teacher in the classroom, then as a teacher trainer, and then as the coordinator and curriculum developer. I learned a lot from being submissive. I never said 'no', and that helped me to grow. Then when I became chief of the foreign teachers, I was able to do things my way, especially with the new high school programme. I designed lesson plans where English would be taught in English. I wanted students to hear English more and to enjoy English – that's why action and gesture is so important. I guess I wanted to teach English the way I was taught in the Philippines.

After working at Shogakan for 17 years, I left to go back to the Philippines to finish my MA in education, but I had to come back before completing because my father-in-law passed away and I'd promised him I would look after my mum-in-law. So then I started working for Saitama Board of Education as an ALT, because the hours suited me better.

Why did I start FETJ? At the time I was ETJ coordinator in Saitama. I noticed that the other Filipinos didn't take an active part in these meetings. I said, 'Why don't you speak up?' And they said, 'We feel that we don't have the right to speak out in front of native speakers'. 'OK, in that case, let's have our own group to encourage Filipino teachers'. At first, I was just inviting teachers to my home. 'I'm free on Sundays, we'll have a study group meeting'. So they came and asked, 'How do I pronounce this? How do I teach this? What do I do?' But then so many people were coming, I thought I cannot do this alone. So we registered FETJ with the Philippines Embassy. And it grew from there: we have groups now all over Kanto: Kanagawa, Chiba, Tokyo, and soon there's a new one starting in Nagoya. We have over 500 members on our mailing list, perhaps 300 or so of them are active. We have workshops for different seasons, Halloween and Christmas; we have workshops for grammar teaching, for computer skills.

My intention was always just to help my fellow Filipinos. Yes, I do this kind of thing for other groups too: some Japanese ask me for training, but I ask them for money. My work with FETJ is for free. Nowadays, we have other nationalities coming to the workshops. A Hawaiian guy took our certificate course recently and now teaches at a kindergarten.

Aurora's narrative features a number of aspects that are of relevance to her language teacher identity: among those that I notice are her linguistic identity, as a multilingual who received her education through English in the Philippines; her professional identity, starting out in the Philippines as a television broadcaster and then a university teacher in speech and communication, before moving to Japan, where she began her successful career as an English teacher; and her gendered identity as a wife, seemingly subservient to her Japanese husband who ruled which job she could do, and subsequently constrained her choice of job because of her role as primary carer for her mother-in-law.

However, it is the statements that index Aurora's national and ethnic identity that are of most interest to me. Proud of her linguistic heritage, she is nevertheless ambivalent in defining her linguistic identity (*'Am I a native English speaker? That depends on how other people consider me and my English'*). The question and her answer to it can be viewed in different ways: She has already said that English is one of her languages, thus 'other people' could be a challenge to me, her interlocutor, an English woman, and someone who might be expected to harbour prejudiced views about Filipinos teaching English. At the same time, 'other people' could mean her fellow Filipinos, not all of whom will have had access to the same quality of education that she enjoyed. More likely, 'other people' could also mean Japanese people: her employers, the Japanese English teachers with whom she works as an assistant language teacher (ALT) and her students. When Aurora is hired in her first teaching job in Japan at Shogakan, she draws attention to the fact that she was the 'first non-native there'. Being Filipino has never held Aurora back in her career as an English teacher. But that is clearly not true for the Filipinos who felt unable to participate in English Teachers in Japan (ETJ) (*'We feel that we don't have the right to speak out in front of native speakers'*).

To understand the sense of discrimination that is being expressed here, and indeed to understand why Aurora felt motivated to help other Filipino teachers, it is worth examining the historical context that brought many Filipinos to Japan from the 1980s onwards. Both Japan and the Philippines have been undergoing gradual, but profound changes, some of which have been brought about by the effects of 'late capitalism' (Duchêne & Heller, 2012; Mandel, 1972). Career possibilities for Filipinos in Japan have changed in the past few decades, and in the following sections, three significant factors that have led to these shifts are explored in some detail: Filipino migration to Japan, English education in Japan and ideologies about language and culture in Japan.

Filipinos in Japan

Japan and the Philippines are both archipelagoes and, like other island nations, their history of seafaring contact stretches back centuries. Up until the end of the 20th century, contact between Japan and the Philippines was predominantly one way. From the 12th century, Japanese merchants went to the Philippines for pottery and gold. In the 16th century, as the Spanish colonised the Philippine islands, Japanese Christians arrived, with many settling in the area south of Manila that was known as Dilao, meaning yellow in Tagalog (*dilaw*). Many more came as a result of the interdiction of Christianity by the shogunate in the early 17th century, including a samurai, Takayama Ukon, who refused to abandon his faith and went into exile in the Philippines with 300 followers. Beatified in 2017 by Pope Francis, Takayama Ukon's statue still stands in a square in Paco, as the Dilao district is now called. During Spanish rule, many Japanese migrants intermarried with Filipinos, Chinese or Spanish to form a class of mestizos. In the early years of the 20th century, a new layer of Japanese immigrants was added when Japanese migrants were hired as labourers for a major road project in the north of Luzon, followed by yet another wave of migrants who came to work on plantations on the southern island of Mindanao. The descendants of these 20th-century migrants are regarded in Japan as *nikkeijin*, a term that is applied to 'people of Japanese descent living outside Japan, including those who have returned or emigrated to Japan' (Ohno, 2007: 243).

Since the 1990s, Japan has eased its immigration rules to grant up to third-generation *nikkeijin* long-term visas to make up a shortfall of employment in industry and care of the elderly for its increasingly ageing population. In the first decade of this policy, the majority of *nikkeijin* came from Latin American countries, such as Brazil and Peru. Far fewer came from Asian countries, although there are sizeable Japanese diasporas in China and the Philippines. One reason for this, in the case of the Philippines, is that many Japanese migrants had destroyed any documents testifying to their nationality and many had changed their names after the Second World War. Although many local Japanese supported the guerrilla resistance to the Japanese occupation during the war, there was widespread suspicion of collaboration (Ohno, 2007). By 2000, Japanese immigration rules were changed again to ease admission for Filipinos without original documentation, leading to a large-scale influx of *nikkeijin*, supported by 'foundations' and brokers who could facilitate the documentation process and placement in employment in Japan (Vilog, 2013). By 2008, Filipino *nikkeijin* were the second-largest *nikkeijin* population, after Chinese (Ohno, 2008). According to Ohno and Iijima (2010), most Filipino *nikkeijin* continued to stay in Japan for over 10 years on long-term visas or as permanent residents.

Prior to the arrival of Filipino *nikkeijin*, however, large numbers of Filipinos, mostly women, entered Japan as 'entertainers' during the 1980s, and it is this category of migrant that has contributed most to the sexualised stereotype of Filipino women as *japayuki* or *japayukisan*, as they came to be called in the Japanese media (Lie, 2001). Deriving from the Japanese *karayukisan*, literally meaning *Miss China-bound*, which was used to refer to young women from poverty-stricken rural areas who were sent as prostitutes to China and other countries before the Second World War, the association of Filipino women with prostitution was evident from the outset. During Japan's economic 'bubble era' in the 1970s, the Philippines became a popular destination for sex tourism. However, following several well-publicised attacks on Japanese businessmen in Manila, the numbers of Japanese tourists to the Philippines declined, while the numbers of Filipino women entering Japan as tourists increased dramatically, many with the support of criminal gangs in Japan (Oishi, 2005). In 1981, 'entertainer' was added to the restricted list of employment categories for migrants, leading to an influx of thousands of women arriving to work. Most of these were employed in the legal sex industry known as *mizu-shōbai*, or water trade. Prostitution is illegal in Japan, but many women are employed in bars to flirt with customers. Large numbers of Filipino women who came to Japan, whether as tourists or entertainers, stayed on, some legally as spouses of Japanese men they married, but many others illegally as they failed to return to the Philippines when their visas expired. A clampdown on illegal migrants was launched in the 1990s, and tighter stipulation of the professional qualification of entertainers was introduced, making it much harder for Filipinos to enter Japan under that scheme (Oishi, 2005).

In a separate development, the 1990s also saw Filipinos coming to Japan as brides, particularly for men living in depopulated rural areas. A 'bride famine' in the countryside led many municipalities to organise tours to the Philippines and other South East Asian countries to meet potential partners (Umeda, 2009). Although a law was passed in the Philippines in 1990 banning 'mail-order brides', various agencies and media continued to advertise Filipino wives for Japanese men. Reaching a peak of 12,150 in 2006, the number of Japanese-Filipino marriages fell to 3,118 in 2013, but remained the second-largest proportion of international marriages, after Japanese-Chinese (Ministry of Health, Labour and Welfare, n.d.).

Migration for work has been a state policy of the Philippines for the past 40 years. Under President Ferdinand Marcos, a new labour code was promulgated in 1974 that cut wages to 75% of the basic minimum and banned labour action, forcing people to seek work overseas. The code stipulated that a portion of Filipino overseas workers' foreign exchange remittances to relatives in the Philippines would be sequestered to help ease a balance of payments crisis (Tyner, 2004). Although labour migration globally is undertaken predominantly by men, in the case of the Philippines the vast majority of migrants are women (Parrenas, 2008), who work in affluent countries as domestic workers, nannies and carers, categories of employment that are not permitted for immigration to Japan.

More recently, the type of work that Filipino migrants undertake has changed. Whereas, previously, Filipinos in Japan were accepted only as 'entertainers' or for '3Ds' work, i.e. 'dirty, dangerous and demeaning' (referred to in Japanese as the 3Ks: *kitanai, kiken, kitsui*), they are now coming in greater numbers to occupy skilled labour positions. In 2018, Filipinos comprised the third-largest group of trainees on government internship programmes for technical and care work. In 1993, a technical intern training programme was implemented, ostensibly to contribute to the international community by relaying Japanese skills to developing countries. After a year-long training, participants were permitted to stay for a further two years of on-the-job 'training'. Subject to widespread abuse, the scheme was criticised for its violation of labour regulations, such as unpaid overtime. Despite revision of the law in 2010 to protect foreign trainees, in May 2014 a Filipino man died as a result of overwork at the company in Gifu where he was training (Rappler, 2016). With further regulations in place to ensure compliance by employers, the scheme has been expanded. In addition, the immigration law has been amended to include care workers who are desperately needed to cope with the demands of Japan's ageing society.

Overall, the number of Filipinos entering Japan has continued to rise incrementally since the 1990s, with Filipinos occupying third place in the

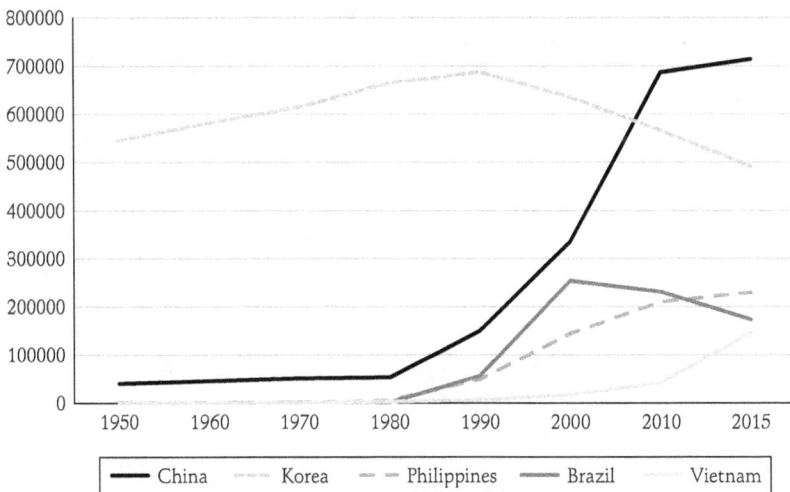

Figure 2.1 Registered foreigners by nationality: 1950–2015 (Source: Ministry of Justice, Statistics on the foreigners registered in Japan; see www.ipss.go.jp/p-info/e/psj2017/PSJ2017-10.xls)

proportion of foreigner residents, numbering 229,595 out of a total of 2.23 million in 2015 (Murai, 2016), although 2019 figures indicate that Vietnamese have now outstripped Filipinos to become the third-largest group (Osumi, 2019). Whereas Koreans originally accounted for the vast majority of foreign residents in Japan, their numbers have fallen dramatically, as Koreans have assimilated and taken Japanese citizenship, or in some cases returned to Korea (Green, 2017). Although Japan has never been as homogeneous as popular belief would have it (Maher & Yashiro, 1995), the increase in new migrants from South East Asia, a significant proportion of whom are Filipino, means that Japan has quietly (Green, 2017) but visibly become more multicultural over the past few decades, as the graph in Figure 2.1 illustrates. With the passing of a law to admit 345,000 more foreign workers from neighbouring countries at the end of 2018, the shift to a more multicultural Japan can only accelerate.

English Language Education in Japan

Just as migration policy in Japan has fluctuated according to real and perceived needs in any given period, so too language and language education policy has changed over time. When the Meiji era (1868–1912) brought an end to Japan's more than 200-year isolation from the world, a period of rapid modernisation began in which the technical and military achievements of the West were vaunted as ideals. Foreign specialists were invited to lecture on their subjects and their words were translated into Japanese for the benefit of those attending the lectures and readers. The first Minister for Education Arinori Mori promoted the learning of English above other languages as English-speaking countries carried greater power economically. As Japan grew stronger, and particularly as it rode on the successes of its wars with China (1894–1895) and Russia (1904–1905), reliance on foreign teachers and translation came to be seen as unnecessary and unpatriotic. Instead, education policy came to be guided by the slogan 'Education in Japan in Japanese' and by the 1930s, English education was largely abandoned.

After Japan's defeat in the Second World War and during a seven-year period of occupation by the United States, there was a 'boom' in English learning (Butler & Iino, 2005), and English was included in the curriculum of the new education system as a compulsory subject in the three years of junior high school. English was also set as an integral part of university entrance examinations, and thus English was also required *de facto* in the three years of senior high school. By the end of the 1980s, as Japan's bubble burst and it entered into a period of economic stagnation, many regarded English education as the cause of, as well as the solution to its ills. As successive governments called for greater 'internationalisation' (*kokusaika*) to revive economic growth, an 'Action Plan to Develop Japanese with English Abilities' was drawn up and launched in 2003. The focus of English education was intended to be on practical communicative skills, although in practice the prescribed textbooks continued to adhere basically to a grammar syllabus.

A central plank of the communicative English policy has been the introduction of foreign teachers in the English classrooms. In 1987, the Education Ministry and the Ministry of Foreign Affairs launched a joint venture called the Japan Exchange and Teaching (JET) programme. More than 30 years later, the scheme is regarded as a mixed success. Participants are recruited for a period of one year, with the option to renew for up to five years, to one of three roles: the vast majority of JETs work as ALTs, while a smaller number work as coordinators for international relations (CIRs) in city and regional government offices and a handful work as sports coordinators. Initially intended to allay trade tensions with the United States, the JET programme has been largely successful in its diplomatic initiative of generating goodwill in Japan's international relations (Metzgar, 2017) and introducing diversity to schools and communities throughout Japan (McConnell, 2000). But continued criticisms have been voiced throughout the life of this scheme: from Japanese teachers about cultural and language barriers with JET assistants, and from JETs, that they are limited to the role of human 'tape recorders' (McCrostie, 2017).

The JET programme hit a peak of 6273 in 2002 (JET Programme, n.d.), falling by one-third in 2010 before increasing again to 5761 in 2019. The majority of the 5234 ALTs who participated in the programme in 2019 came from the United States (2958), followed by Canada (531), the United Kingdom (528), Australia (321) and New Zealand (236). In 2014, for the first time two Filipinos were accepted as ALTs on the JET programme. In 2019, 136 ALTs came from the Philippines, the same number as were invited from South Africa (JET Programme, n.d.).

The change in attitudes towards Filipinos as potential English teachers by the JET programme follows a trend that has been apparent for more than a decade in the private sector. In fact, currently less than a quarter of the ALTs deployed in public junior high and high schools, and since 2011 in elementary schools too, are from the JET programme. The majority of ALTs are now hired directly by local boards of education or by dispatch agencies.

Dispatch agencies (*haken gaisha*) have come to play a major role in the recruitment and deployment of ALTs since an amendment to the Workers Dispatch Law (*rodosha haken ho*) in 1999. The deregulation enabled private agencies to tender for contracts to supply teachers to schools. According to a 2009 survey, most boards of education preferred dispatch ALTs to JETs because of paperwork and cost (Sato, 2012). According to Currie-Robson (2015: 255), 'JETs earn over $40,000 a year; by sending their instructors in bulk, and offering lower pay and benefits, dispatch agencies can charge around $30,000 a year and keep a third of that'. Dispatch companies, along with private English conversation (*eikaiwa*) schools, have been accused of short-changing teachers by employing them on contracts of 29.5 hours per week, just under the 30-hour level above which they would be obliged to pay benefits such as health insurance. Currie-Robson (2015) traces a steady worsening of pay and conditions by dispatch companies and *eikaiwas* in an occupation that used to be regarded as high paid and high status but is now seen increasingly as low paid and precarious. One consequence of this downgrading of the salaries and conditions of ALT work is that it has driven away many teachers from countries such as the United States and the United Kingdom that were traditionally favoured as a source of English teachers, and opened the door for Filipinos to teach in schools.

English education in schools has long been regarded as a fit target for condemnation, with Japan consistently ranking near the bottom in standardised tests of English compared with other countries. A grammar-based curriculum (in spite of the supposed emphasis on communication) and a focus on school tests and university entrance examinations are commonly blamed for the national shortcoming. However, another school of thought sees communicative ability as something that is outside the remit of school education. Japanese who want to use English – whether for business or pleasure – have enrolled in large numbers in the *eikaiwas*. According to Otake (2004), in 2002 *eikaiwa* was a 670 billion yen industry, with the five biggest chains (Nova, Aeon, GEOS, ECC and Berlitz) accounting for 25%. Through the anecdotes of teachers who worked in these schools, the picture that is conjured by Currie-Robson (2015) is one of McDonaldised systems of standardised product (teaching materials and 'blond, blue-eyed teachers') and rapacious marketing.

With the bankruptcy of Nova in 2007, the *eikaiwa* bubble was deflated, as clients left for smaller schools with a more personalised touch. However, even before 2007 and increasingly since then, small English conversation schools and studios, often comprising a single teacher, have come to form a vast 'cottage industry' (Nagatomo, 2016). Nagatomo (2016) has noted how these small schools offer an outlet and an income for foreign wives of Japanese men. Her study focused only on women from Inner-Circle countries (Kachru, 1985), but women from other countries, especially the Philippines, have been starting small businesses too. Apart from the decline in the large corporate *eikaiwas*, a further impetus for foreign women to open English schools has undoubtedly been the lowering of the age for compulsory English from 12 to 10 in 2011. An English education 'reform plan corresponding to globalisation' sees the age further lowered to the age of eight from 2020 (MEXT, 2017), thus bringing Japan's English education policy into line with that of South Korea and China. In elementary school, children engage in 'foreign language activities', the aim of which is 'to form the foundation of pupils' communication abilities through foreign languages while developing an understanding of languages and cultures through various experiences, fostering a positive attitude toward communication, and familiarising pupils with the sounds and basic expressions of foreign languages' (MEXT, 2017). The MEXT policy document advocates that English be used 'in principle' for foreign language activities but avoids associating English with any particular country or identity, opening up possibilities that did not exist previously for English speakers from countries outside the Inner Circle (Kachru, 1985), such as the Philippines.

Supplementary classes outside of school are hugely popular in Japan, not so much as a way to make up or catch up with content in school classes but as a way to give children an advantage. Lowering the age of English in school means lowering the age at which children will take English classes outside of school, so that they have an edge over their peers. As we will see in the following chapters, FETJ places most emphasis on teaching English to such young and very young learners.

Language Teacher Ideologies

Filipinos have entered Japan in substantial and increasing numbers over the past 30 years at a time when Japan has suffered from a stagnating economy, an increasingly precariatised workforce (Osawa & Kingston, 2010) and a shrinking population. These economic and demographic challenges, following Japan's boom years after the Second World War, have led to a protracted ideological divide on how Japanese people see themselves in the world. Officially, internationalisation (*kokusaika*) has been seen as the key to recovery ever since the onset of the decline, though what that might mean or entail has been subject to debate and resistance. Kubota (1999, 2002) has argued persuasively that, in terms of education policy in the 1980s and 1990s, interpretations of internationalisation were coloured by nationalistic stereotypes of Japanese cultural homogeneity and of other cultures, an ideology known as *nihonjinron*, or theories/discussions about the Japanese.

Blommaert (2005: 164) defines ideology as 'materially mediated ideational phenomena', emphasising the fact that material structures and resources are deployed to create and maintain a status quo that is of benefit to some more than others. At the same time, shifts in the global economic order have led to new, often contradictory relations of power on macro and micro levels (Blommaert, 2015). This is apparent in Japan, in ideological contradictions in English language curricula, in teaching materials and teaching practices and in hiring policies. Thus, textbooks that continue to emphasise grammar over communication have made top-down directives to schools on communicative language teaching (CLT) and active learning virtually impossible. An ideological contradiction is also apparent between the Japanese state's aspiration to mould internationally minded, linguistically and culturally competent citizens, and the reality of an underfunded school system where foreign ALTs are shared between multiple schools (Luxton *et al.*, 2014). It is apparent too in the massive private sector of *eikaiwas* and cram schools, or *jukus*, where parents must pay for their children's educational achievement.

The perception and value of multilingual education in practice is thus highly stratified in Japanese society. Kanno's (2008) excellent ethnographic study of five schools in Japan that claim to offer a bilingual education provides a stark illustration of how class and race are implicated in the valuing of languages and the substantial investment of time and money required to acquire them. The elite international school in her study provides support for Japanese children's English development, but at home mothers push their children to work on their Japanese to ensure that their proficiency does not fall behind that of children educated in mainstream Japanese schools. Meanwhile, the multilingual abilities of children of Asian immigrants in low-status jobs are not recognised or valued in the provincial public schools that Kanno observed, and resources that would help develop their Japanese, and hence their future success in Japan, appear to be inadequate. Whereas bilingualism is regarded as cumulative in the case of the English-dominant elite international school students, it is regarded as a deficit for the children of poorer migrants in a public school outside Tokyo. The failure of such children in the Japanese education system has tended to be attributed to the children themselves and their families, rather than to any shortcomings of the system (Kanno, 2008).

Ideologies are thus mediated through material resources, such as language curricula or investment of time and money in language education. They are also implicated in language teacher identity. Hayes (2013) has argued that language teacher identity is 'dichotomised' in the Japanese public education system. Teachers are classed as civil servants and, as such, the job of 'teacher' is reserved exclusively for Japanese. Foreigners, classed as 'native speakers', are hired merely to lend support to Japanese teachers. This was not always the case. Hashimoto (2013) shows that British and North American teachers were invited to work as teachers in Japan prior to the inauguration of the JET programme. However, participants in the JET programme were classified as assistants to Japanese English teachers, a demotion that is even more apparent in the discrepancy between the English term assistant language *teacher* and the original Japanese term *gaikokugo shidou* joshu or language teaching *assistant*. Whereas previously invited foreign teachers employed their own pedagogies, the current practice of team teaching requires ALTs to fit in with Japanese educational practices, and thus, Hashimoto argues, negates the JET programme's avowed aim of internationalisation.

Houghton and Rivers (2013) argue that in Japan such practices embody a particular form of 'native-speakerism'. Coined by Holliday (2005, 2006) to refer to a form of uncritical thinking that legitimises Anglo-Saxon prejudice against non-native speakers from outside the English-speaking West, native-speakerism can also thrive within non-Western and non-English-speaking contexts (Houghton & Rivers, 2013). Thus, in Japan, it takes the form of chauvinism, manifested in *nihonjinron* ideology that portrays Japan as racially and culturally homogeneous, disregarding the existence of various ethnic groups living there (Maher & Yashiro, 1995). From this perspective, it is the 'native-speaker' English teachers who become the target of pervasive prejudice and marginalisation, and this, Houghton and Rivers argue, makes it a human rights issue. Accordingly, they propose an amended definition of 'native-speakerism' as

> prejudice, stereotyping and/or discrimination, typically by or against foreign language teachers, on the basis of either being or not being perceived and categorized as a native speaker of a particular language, which can form part of a larger complex of inter-connected prejudices including ethnocentrism, racism and sexism. Its endorsement positions individuals from certain language groups as being innately superior to individuals from other language groups. Therefore, native-speakerist policies and practices represent a fundamental breach of one's human rights. (Houghton & Rivers, 2013: 14)

The thrust of this argument serves to challenge the more widespread assumption that native-speakerism is specifically White and colonialist (Kubota & Lin, 2011; Motha, 2014; Swan *et al.*, 2015; Vandrick, 1999). As we saw in Aurora's observation that she was the first non-native teacher to be hired by Shogakan, English speakers from outside the Inner Circle were not commonly considered to be 'native speakers' in the early 1990s when she first started working there.

However, such critical assessments of the ideologies surrounding English and English education in Japan overlook the (admittedly slow) changes in society and in the education system. For many years, the nationalist ideology of *nihonjinron* has conflicted with an ideology of *kokusaika* or internationalisation (Kubota, 1999, 2002), a conflict that has surely slowed the pace of change in Japan. Nevertheless, change is occurring. In addition to the recruitment in recent years of Filipinos onto the JET programme, two universities have explicitly based their English curricula on the principles of English as a lingua franca (Tamagawa University) and World Englishes (Chubu University), which has led to the appointment of more diverse faculty in those universities. This trend is reflected in many other universities too that have adopted English-medium instruction (EMI) in order to meet the official goal of significantly increasing the number of international students (Ota & Horiuchi, 2018). In addition, as I mentioned earlier, the dispatch companies, which now supply the majority of English language ALTs to public schools, started recruiting Filipinos and other South Asians in the early 2000s. This shift in institutions' attitudes towards Filipinos may be driven, at least in part, by more enlightened ideologies concerning language and language teacher identity. However, as Hashimoto has shown in her critical analysis of government policy regarding ALTs, competing ideologies may lead to contradiction and ambiguity in practice.

Historically constituted, the ideologies of *nihonjinron* and *kokusaika* are directly opposed, but they are also interconnected. *Nihonjinron* and the 'allergic' attitudes it engenders towards English and English speakers (Houghton *et al.*, 2018) belong to a wider set of beliefs that is the product of, and in service to, a world view and a political economic system that is based on national sovereignty, and hence national particularity. In the same way, *kokusaika* and multilingualism belong to a wider set of beliefs associated with globalisation. As a phenomenon, globalisation has been defined as a 'transformation in the spatial organisation of social relations and transactions assessed in terms of their extensity, intensity, velocity and impact' (Held *et al.*, 1999: 68), a transformation that takes the form of flows of people, products, capital and information. However, to the extent that it is driven by the quest for profit, globalisation also reflects an ideological view and a political economic system that has been referred to (mainly by its critics) as *neoliberalism*.

Since the collapse of the Soviet Union in 1991, and despite the global financial crisis of 2008, neoliberalism has become the dominant political economic system worldwide, or as the journalist Martin Jacques (2016) put it in an article for *The Guardian* newspaper, 'politically and intellectually, the only show in town'. Like any ideology, this system also exerts shaping influences on individual identity. These influences will be explored in Chapter 3 in the narratives of two teachers, Lori and Elma, with a particular focus on the role that economic metaphors have played in conceptualising language learner and teacher identity. I will argue that, just as identity is shaped by prevailing political economic structures and ideologies, so too this economic view of identity is influenced by the same ideological assumptions.

3 Investment and Recognition

In Chapter 2, Aurora's story provided a launching point for a consideration of the changing contexts – social, educational and ideological – in which English teachers work in Japan. The narratives included in this book cover a long period of time, from the mid-1980s to 2017, and thus the lives and work of older teachers who have been in Japan for decades are shaped by contextual conditions in quite different ways to the relative newcomers. In this chapter, I present the stories of two women who have lived in Japan since the early 1990s and mid-1980s, respectively. Their stories contain vivid examples of how their intersectional identities (Block & Corona, 2016; Crenshaw, 1989, 1991) – not only their ethnicity, but also their gender, occupation, marital status and age – have at times made them vulnerable to prejudice, which they describe in their stories of becoming and being English teachers in Japan. But the stories also illustrate how they overcame prejudice, both through their own accomplishments and success and as part of collective endeavours through their involvement with Filipino English Teacher in Japan (FETJ) and other Filipino associations.

A particular aspect that I want to discuss in this chapter is the notion of investment, a theme that, in different ways, runs through the two narratives. Investment has been taken up by a number of researchers following the influential work of Bonny Norton, whose use of this economic metaphor draws on the social theory of Pierre Bourdieu. Although I do not deny the literal investment that these teachers make in their teaching lives, I wish to problematise its use as a metaphor for conceptualising identity. My argument builds on the discussion I started in Chapter 2 on the ideology of neoliberalism and concludes by considering alternative concepts that I believe are more closely aligned to theories of recognition.

I begin with Lori's story. I met Lori in 2010 at a conference in Saitama where I first came across FETJ. Lori was giving a presentation, along with Aurora, on the work of FETJ. She was with her partner and their toddler, who kept running up to hug her mother's knees during her presentation. Lori seemed much younger and less confident than Aurora, and I was surprised when I later discovered in 2012, as we chatted before she started telling her story, that she was only a few years younger, already in her mid-40s. Before she started telling her story, she expressed some anxiety about her English, although I did not feel that she had any cause to feel anxious.

Lori's Story

I come from a middle-class family in Manila. There were eight of us kids and all but one of us went to college. When I was young, my dream was to be a doctor, so I took the pre-medical course at university. If I had stayed another four years, I could have become a doctor, but my sister moved to Japan and married a Japanese at that time, and she convinced me to come to Japan too.

This was the early 90s, and in those days teaching jobs weren't available to Filipinos. So I got work in a factory and in a snack bar. I learned to speak Japanese there, as the job was to serve the customers drinks and chat to them. Then I met a man, a Japanese, and had a baby. We didn't get married, but, because I had a child, I could get a long-term visa. As a single mother, I carried on working part time, in the factory and at night in a snack bar.

Then, when my son went to kindergarten, a Filipino friend of mind suggested starting an English class. We planned it together and started renting a room in a community centre. It was really cheap, just 500 yen per day, and we charged 500 yen for each child. At first, this job didn't give me anything. My friend was the one who set it up, actually. I was afraid to talk to the mothers. I felt that they wouldn't approve of me because of my work in the evenings. Also, I'm shy but my friend was really good at Japanese and at PR. So she took all the money at first. She just gave me pocket money from it, and I just did it for the experience. I was thinking that this could be my 'bread and butter': This could be a better job for me in the future.

So when I started teaching, I was still working at the snack bar at night and teaching in the afternoon. After kindergarten, the mothers would bring their kids and I would teach them in groups of eight, one hour per class, though the last 15 minutes of the class was just colouring. We didn't promote it with flyers or pamphlets or anything, but little by little the number of students increased so that after two years I was teaching 200 students. Incredible, isn't it? Monday to Saturday three or four classes per day.

Actually, before then I could earn quite a lot of money working in the snack bar, especially compared with something like working in a factory. But I always felt, 'I can do better than this'. Still, at that time, I didn't have a choice, I had to earn money for me and my son. So then I started to make enough money from teaching, and more mothers were coming to me and asking me to teach their children.

To tell the truth, I didn't know very much about teaching at that time. I was trying my best, and giving my best, but I didn't know anything about methods or techniques. So I started attending seminars whenever I could. I even went down to Hiroshima for a one-week seminar. I attended a TESOL seminar in Kanagawa, which cost 100,000 yen, and the Nakata seminar, which was 40,000 for just two days. But I got certificates from attending these courses, and I gained a lot of confidence and knowledge.

I was finally able to lose my fear, my sense of inferiority, at Harry Cotton's seminar in Kanagawa. Before that, I was afraid to speak or perform in front of a group. I was afraid to talk about my classes. Even when I was in Hiroshima, I couldn't speak up. The other participants were mainly native speakers and I felt left out. English is their language and they are really outspoken. I felt that I wasn't at the same level as them. And then I had a bad experience with this American woman. We were team teaching and the student was joking around saying 'How old is the teacher?' And I was joking and laughing too. She got really mad and said, 'Don't make fun of me'. But I realised that you can't teach with that attitude. You can't take yourself so seriously in front of the children. So that was Hiroshima in 2002. But by 2005 Kanagawa seminar, I was much more confident.

I was also involved in the Filipino English Teacher in Japan association, which started in Omiya in 2000. At first, I was just a participant in the workshops and I learned a lot about techniques and teaching materials. Then, in 2004, a missionary friend of mine asked me if I would run a similar workshop for women from the Philippines, like me, who wanted to become teachers. Our goal was to give women another choice in their lives, so they could get more self-esteem and be more accepted in Japan. I was doing that for two years, and then our group merged with FETJ and I was asked to be a trainer of teachers for FETJ. FETJ was starting to get really big. New chapters were opening in different places, and more and more teachers came each time.

More Filipino teachers were starting to get jobs in schools and I decided I wanted to get one too. I had been teaching by myself for several years and I felt it was time to move on and grow. I was giving seminars for FETJ and was sharing what I knew about teaching, but I didn't know anything about working as an ALT. I wanted to know about schools and I knew that working together with a Japanese teacher I would have to improve myself.

My first job was at an elementary school. The really different thing was making detailed lesson plans: I have to explain each topic and then submit and discuss it with the homeroom teacher. That was a very good experience. I felt, 'Now I'm really a teacher!' The teacher was very encouraging and asked me to do everything in the class. But at the end of the year – actually, just one day before the start of the new year – the *agency I was working for said they didn't have a contract with the school for the next year so that was the end of the job. I immediately applied to other agencies and got a job with IES at a junior high school. This time it was a six-month contract and the recruitment manager said, 'If you do a good job it will be renewed no problem'. I was quite reassured because I felt confident that I could do a good job in the classroom. So it came as a shock when they said the contract wouldn't be renewed. It wasn't because I was no good, it was because the school only had a budget for ALTs for six months. So in the middle of the year, I had to scramble for another job. There were a lot of other teachers in the same situation, who had thought they were signing up to something more permanent.*

In my case, luckily, my friend told me that there was an opening at the BoE (Board of Education) and I applied and got the job. So I've been working there now for five months and have a contract for next year. The conditions are much better than at the agency: the hours are shorter and the pay is more. I now work at a junior high school and two elementary schools, so I'm at a different school each day, and I like the variety. Another good thing about this job is that I get to teach solo in the junior high school as well as the elementary school. When I was working for IES, I was just an ALT, I just sat at the back of the class, and the Japanese teacher did all the teaching.

But to be honest, I don't enjoy the junior high school classes so much. The kids are teenagers and shy and they don't want to speak up, unlike younger kids. Also, we have to use a textbook, which is too difficult for them. I have to follow it, but I try to simplify the tasks for them, or give them games so the class doesn't die. But at the moment, for example, we have to do a debate, and it's really impossible.

I'm still very busy with FETJ. There are more and more possibilities for Filipino teachers, especially since the earthquake, and many of them start with us, then, after they get jobs, continue to come to support the group and to support new teachers. The other day I was at a meeting of the BoE for ALTs and about 80% of the teachers there were Filipino.

Lori's story vividly illustrates both the changing social context that I described in Chapter 2, and the growing confidence that she comes to feel in herself as an English teacher. Coming to Japan in the early 1990s when job opportunities were limited mainly to 'entertainment' in bars and factory work, Lori's career as an English teacher starts when her son goes to kindergarten. Although Lori is 'afraid to talk to the mothers', sensitive to what she fears may be their prejudiced perception of her as a Filipino bar worker and single mother, and lacking the confidence to speak for herself, it is as a kindergarten mother herself that she gains access to opportunities for teaching work, as her more outspoken Filipino friend clearly recognised. Despite her obvious success in this venture, attracting 200 students to her English classes, Lori nevertheless felt 'a sense of inferiority' in the company of 'native speaker' English teachers at the teacher training seminars that she paid large sums to attend. She is able to overcome these fears by the Kanagawa seminar she attended 2005, having built up her confidence not only through her teaching experience, but also through her work with the fledgling FETJ group and the workshops with the missionary worker. Lori's career trajectory has led her to work in public schools as an assistant language teacher (ALT), first with a dispatch agency, which fails to provide her with job security, and subsequently with a BoE. Moving to school teaching, however, despite the precarious nature of her agency work, gives her a stronger sense of identity as a teacher ('*Now I'm really a teacher!*').

Prejudice and pride are evident at various points throughout Lori's narrative. Apart from one upsetting episode at the Hiroshima seminar when an American fellow participant reprimands her for joking and making fun of her in their role play, social prejudice is conveyed in Lori's feelings of fear and sense of inferiority, and these feelings have the effect of stopping her from speaking to the mothers or speaking back to the American seminar participant or from taking part in professional development seminars with native speakers for the three-year period between the Hiroshima and Kanagawa seminars. Lori takes pride in her personal success with the kindergarten English classes and in the growing prominence of Filipinos in public school English education in Japan, noting that 80% of the ALTs at her recent BoE meeting were Filipinos.

A notion of investment is also apparent in Lori's narrative. Money, especially, is a recurrent theme in this story, for example, the need to earn a living, the profits she could make from teaching kindergarteners and the cost of the teacher development seminars she attended. Before going on to discuss the problems of conceptualising identity as investment or self-investment, I present Elma Cruz, a Filipino woman in her early 60s, who has been a leading member of FETJ in the Kansai region of Japan. Although I met Elma briefly at an FETJ event some years previously, it was only in 2017 that I asked her to tell me her story for this book, which she did in a long Skype call. Elma's life in Japan started a few years before Lori's; like Aurora and Lori, Elma has lived through the period of change in the field of English teaching in Japan that I described in Chapter 2.

Elma's Story

I came to Japan first in 1985 as a tourist. I had graduated from the Philippine School of Business Administration where I had been teaching marketing and management. My co-teacher Marie and I took a trip to Japan together. She had family in Japan, two sisters who were married to Japanese, and at that time it was not too difficult to get a visa. So we came for 30 days and while we were here we had the chance to do some substitute teaching for a school called Britannica American Village. The school liked us and insisted we do more teaching. It then turned out that they were hiring so we interviewed with them and were accepted. Of course, we'd come on tourist visas, so we had to go back to the Philippines while the school sorted out sponsorship for work visas, but then we returned and started working with Britannica American Village, Marie in Hoshigaoka and I worked in their Nagoya branch.

After six or seven years, the management changed and the school closed down. Marie got hired by Interac, and I got a job with ECC. The head of ECC at the time was a very decent man. He said, normally we don't hire Filipinos, but he saw I had good experience and he gave me the job. As a Filipino I had to prove myself, I had to be better than other teachers. And at ECC I got an award as one of the best teachers. Every year they send out student surveys, and I was among the top three teachers. So after a few years, they started to hire more Filipinos. After 13 years, I heard they had a new policy, that they wanted only younger teachers, and I was asked to change from full time to part time. I felt that this was a signal for me to let go of the job.

I was already 45 by this time and I decided I wanted to leave the city and move to somewhere quieter, so I moved to Nagahama in Shiga, close to Kyoto and Osaka. I got work as an ALT at a girls private school in Otsu. It was quite a long way for me to travel, but I liked it and I stayed there for five years. Now I teach business English classes at a polytechnic college in Shiga twice a week. I also get work from four different dispatch companies and they send me students in the evenings. And I still have one kindergarten where I teach on Friday mornings.

How did I come to be involved with FETJ? Marie told me about it first of all. She said that they were coming to Nagoya to do a Teacher Guidelines Seminar and persuaded me to join her. At first I was unwilling, but since she had asked me, and I thought it would be a good opportunity to meet teachers and aspiring teachers, I went. That's where I met Aurora and she quickly got me involved in presenting and doing training. She encouraged me to start a new Shiga Chapter and whenever she comes to Kansai, she invites me along to do segments of the seminar. FETJ really expanded because of my efforts. I do volunteer work with a lot of different groups. I go to church where I serve as a commentator or doing readings. And I belong to other groups, like the Philippine Coordinating Council in Osaka, so I know a lot of people and it's easy for me to reach out.

Back in the Philippines, I have a Montessori pre-school. In 1996, my mum passed at the age of 56, and I promised her that I would start a school in the Philippines in her name. It would be her legacy. So by 2000 I was planning the school with my siblings: I'm the oldest of five, one brother and three younger sisters. Three of them are now in Japan, and one of them, Ethel, is in the Philippines, working as principal of the Montessori pre-school. We bought two units in a row house in a subdivision in Bulakan near Quezon City. One of the units was a corner plot so we thought it would be good for a school, and that we could provide a service for the families living in the sub-division. Although we were teachers, we had no background in running a school as a business, so we had to learn along the way about hiring staff or obtaining business permits. But we put together a feasibility study, and then in June 2003 we opened the school with just 13 students and two teachers, one working in the morning, the other working in the afternoon. The school did well and reached a peak intake of 65 students and six teachers. I don't know if you know but the Department of Education in the Philippines changed the curriculum to K-12, so enrolment dropped as some parents sent their children to public school instead. But the numbers have gone back up again a little and we are now employing four teachers. The school year in the Philippines runs from June to March and graduation is on March 24th.

So that was my first investment with the money I was earning from teaching in Japan. After working here several years, I was able to invite my brother and sisters out to Japan in 2005. My brother now has a job as marketing manager at a meat processing plant, and my sisters work as English teachers in an international pre-school. Actually, one of them has now moved to Mississippi with her American husband, and we're thinking of starting another Montessori school there.

My work with FETJ involves a lot of coaching, especially at this time of year, when schools are hiring. They come to my home for help in writing their resume, in doing interviews. Most of them come to FETJ because they forgot their English and want to brush it up again, especially grammar. Many college graduates come to Japan and get work as factory workers and they lose their English over time and they don't have confidence. They pay a fee, but it's minimal. If Aurora comes, we need to pay for shinkansen, hotel and food, so we need a minimum of 10 people at a seminar. The participants get a certificate for completing TGS and the grammar course, not for the small practical workshops we do on things like interviewing or resume building. I've done some business English workshops in Okayama and Nagoya and the participants of those got certificates.

I tell the aspiring teachers that they need to focus on personal, professional development and they should try to go to as many seminars as possible. Still a lot of Filipinos assume that the only jobs that are available to them are factory work or, you know, japayuki. When I meet them in church, they are amazed and say, 'How can I be like you?' There used to be a lot of prejudice and discrimination of Filipinos but it was possible to overcome it. Once you show them that you are better than other teachers, they respect you and like you. Of course, it's hard, you need perseverance. I'm not married, and I've been living by myself for all these years, but perhaps that is a good thing as I have been free to work and do different things.

Unlike Lori, Elma was already established as a teacher of marketing and management at college level in the Philippines when she first came to Japan as a tourist with her friend and colleague Marie. Her move to Japan was an enhancement of her social (and economic) status viewed from a Filipino perspective, but a declassing in terms of her professional status in Japan.

Elma is more open than Lori about the topic of prejudice and discrimination. The director of the second school that hired her states baldly that they did not usually hire Filipinos, and thus she recounts that 'as a Filipino I had to prove myself, I had to be better than other teachers'. For Elma, it is a matter of pride that she was able to prove that she was better, by winning awards as one of the best teachers in the school. Despite her success as a teacher, however, her age becomes a further factor that stands against her. A policy change at the school leads her to feel that she has to leave the school. Where she was able to counter prejudicial attitudes towards her as a Filipino, the intersectional effects of being not just Filipino, but an older Filipino serve to multiply the disadvantage that she experiences (Crenshaw, 1989, 1991).

Like Lori, Elma uses her knowledge and expertise as a teacher to help other Filipinos embark on a teaching career. For many Filipinos, Elma is a role model ('*How can we be like you?*'), and her advice to them is to 'show them that you are better than other teachers'. She does not mention here that she took a drop in social status when she came to Japan, but she does suggest that she was only able to succeed in a teaching career in Japan at the expense of marriage and a family. Indeed, Elma's success, the achievement in which she takes pride, is not so much the teaching that she has done in Japan, as it is a family project. Rather than her own teaching career, the pinnacle of her success may be the founding of a Montessori pre-school with her sisters in the Philippines, and bringing her brother and two of her sisters out to Japan where they have had successful careers: in the case of her brother, moving from the factory floor into management in the meat processing factory, and in the case of her sisters, working in international pre-schools, with one of them subsequently moving with her American husband to the United States where she plans to open another Montessori school.

The career paths that Lori and Elma narrate touch on painful episodes where each of them feels their value as a teacher, both potential and actual, is unacknowledged or ignored. Similarly, both teachers recount instances where their professional worth is recognised: for instance, Lori's success in her private teaching and subsequently in being hired by the dispatch company and then by the BoE, and Elma's success as testified by the students' evaluations in the *eikaiwa*. The telling of a career story frames success as an individual achievement; but the role of agency in each of these stories seems more contested than this framing implies. How does this mesh with notions of identity in the literature? In the following sections, I take up two concepts that are highly influential in the literature and research on language teacher identity, investment and desire, before comparing these with the notion of recognition.

Investment

The concept of investment has come to be accepted as a powerful heuristic for understanding identity and identity formation, as can be seen from the extensive literature review in an article by Darvin and Norton (2015). Bonny Norton introduced the term to the field of applied linguistics, specifically second language acquisition, to explain the relative success or failure of women immigrants whose lives in Canada she followed in an ethnographic case study (Norton, 2000, 2013; Norton Peirce, 1995). Norton's thinking about power and its effect on the individual draws inspiration largely from the social theory of Pierre Bourdieu (1977, 1984, 1990, 1991). In Bourdieu's work, power is expressed as an economic metaphor of value through the term *capital*, extending the material sense in which it was originally employed by Marx, to include non-material attributes such as social, cultural and symbolic capital. An investment in learning English, as Norton described the learning efforts of her participants, could be understood as a desire to acquire cultural capital, but progress in this endeavour could be impeded by social conditions, such as in the case of the maid, Saliha, whose access to opportunities to use English was extremely limited, or by an ambivalent desire to learn and practice it, as in the case of Felicia, who resisted being positioned as an immigrant and resented the drop in social status that moving from her native Peru entailed. Subsequently, Norton and others (e.g. Early & Norton, 2014; Tembe & Norton, 2008) have taken the notion of investment to the study of identity in language teachers in Africa, as a way to capture how digital technology is widening the possibilities for imagining what is possible and enabling teachers to increase their cultural capital and social power.

In more recent work, Norton has collaborated with Ron Darvin to develop a model (see Figure 3.1) that links identity to ideology and capital (Darvin & Norton, 2015). As well as learner identity, Norton (2016) has also applied this model to teacher identity.

What the model highlights is the way that an individual's investment is shaped by social forces of ideology and capital. As Darvin and Norton explain:

> It is through an interrogation of ideology that one can examine more closely how power manifests itself materially in the practices of a classroom, workplace, or community; the positioning of interlocutors; and the structuring of habitus. On the other hand, a more fluid conception of capital that recognises how its value shifts across spaces enables a greater

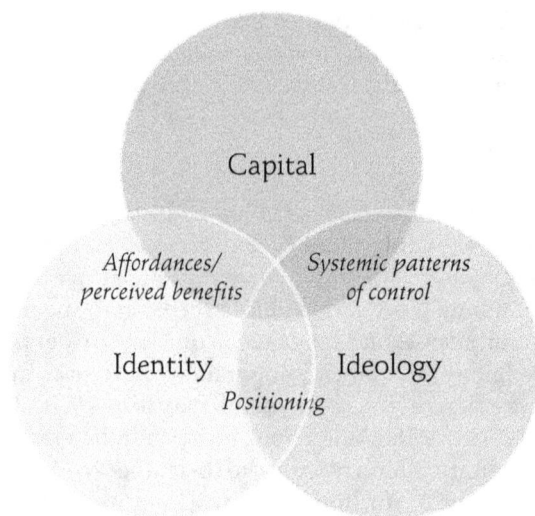

Figure 3.1 Model of investment (From Darvin & Norton, 2015)

understanding of how learners gain or lose power as they lead increasingly mobile lives. (Darvin & Norton, 2015: 42)

Investment, buffeted by fluid capital and ideological power, becomes more or less valuable as an agentive force. This image, based on metaphors of capital and investment, is evocative of a commodity or financial exchange, and I would like to argue that, as such, it is somewhat problematic. Just as the value of an investment rises as an economy prospers and falls as it falters, or is perceived to falter, and particular stocks become attractive or unattractive to investors, so the value of the English language or of Filipino teachers of English might be thought of as fluctuating according to ideological shifts.

As a metaphor to live by (Lakoff & Johnson, 1980), the marketplace has come to permeate thinking about an increasingly wide range of phenomena, including language and identity, in the current era of globalisation and neoliberalism. In the introduction to their anthology of studies that investigate the discourses of 'pride and profit', Monica Heller and Alexandre Duchêne (2012) note that during the late 2000s, in places as far apart as Canada, Switzerland and China's Yunnan Province, they became aware that language and culture were increasingly being talked about in economic terms of 'added value' and 'economic development' rather than merely in terms of national heritage. I would like to suggest that this economic discourse of 'profit' is also apparent in the concept of investment. Darvin and Norton (2015: 46) aver that learners 'invest in particular practices not only because they desire specific material or symbolic benefits, but also because they recognize that the capital they possess can serve as affordances to their learning'. Investment focuses our attention on what learners hope to acquire from their expenditure of money or effort. Individuals are thus construed as managers of their own valuable identities, motivated by self-interest to 'invest' in themselves, so as to maximise and develop various forms of capital.

This is a perspective that appears to correspond to human capital theory, popularised by the Chicago School economist Gary Becker (1964). Becker's theory takes up an idea of human capital proposed by Adam Smith in the 18th century, namely that human capital is similar to physical means of production such as factories or machines. One can invest in human capital by education or training and one's outputs depend partly on the rate of return on the human capital that one owns. Thus, human capital is a means of production into which additional investment yields additional output. Becker has been awarded a Nobel laureate for his work on human capital, but the theory has also drawn harsh criticism for its reification of people, turning them into objects like machines, and for its support of neoliberal ideology (White, 2017).

One of the foremost critics of neoliberalism in the field of language identity is David Block (2014, 2018, Block *et al.*, 2012). Block defines neoliberalism as a means of governance that fundamentally reduces the responsibility of the state towards the individual, and as an ideology by which the individual is seen (and sees themselves) as *homo economicus*, or rational actors. In this light, individuals are regarded as autonomous decision-makers, whose rights and duties as citizens revolve around 'freedom of choice'. But this is a very limited kind of freedom as the choices become limited to the bad and the worse: in 'increasingly precariatized jobs, flexibility imposed from above, being a good consumer, voting in elections for marketized candidates' (Block, 2018: 104). Within this ideology, the neoliberal citizen is also human capital, valued for the skills they possess – or are assumed to possess according to ideologically charged stereotypes, such as the native-speakerist view of English teachers (Holliday, 2005, 2006), or the stereotype of Filipinos as English speaking and endowed with an aptitude for domestic work (Lorente, 2012, 2017). In this view, indeed in the current society, the individual alone is responsible for building their own career and for enhancing their worth through 'self-branding' (Block, 2018).

There is certainly evidence in the narratives that Lori and Elma view their professional identities as human capital. Given the economic insecurity of life as a single mother in Japan, Lori's story in particular brings issues of money and financial stability sharply into focus. She talks in concrete terms about how much it cost to rent the room for her kindergartener English classes, and how much she spent on the teacher training seminars. Lori's first experience of teaching is the small business teaching children from her son's kindergarten, where she is prepared to forego an income at first, accepting just 'pocket money' from her Filipino business partner who had set the classes up. Investment in a teacher identity here is not merely a metaphor.

The significant amounts of time and money invested in becoming a teacher do not bring guaranteed rewards, however. Lori claims that teaching appealed to her as her future 'bread and butter', as a stable job, but in fact, language teachers in the commercial sector, working for dispatch companies, as Lori does when she first becomes an ALT, or *eikaiwa* schools in Elma's case, are far from secure in their employment. Lori's teaching contract is not renewed because the dispatch company she worked for failed to obtain a contract with the BoE. Elma loses her first job when the school goes bankrupt, and is then edged out of her second job because the company wants younger teachers. Rather than her own teaching career, Elma interprets her success as a family project: her achievement in enabling her siblings to move to Japan and opening schools in the Philippines and the United States. These shifts in the way Lori and Elma are valued as teachers, and in the way they themselves value their employment can be explained by shifts in the power structures that govern English teaching in Japan.

Changes in the power structures and ideologies surrounding English teaching in Japan have shifted the goal posts for these two teachers in ways that are both positive and negative. For example, whereas being an English teacher was not an identity that Lori could imagine when she first arrived in Japan in the 1990s, a decade later she *was* able to imagine private English classes for kindergarten children with her Filipino friend and make it a reality. Later, she saw that many Filipinos were starting to obtain work as ALTs and she wanted that for herself too. But these prospects for work as English teachers have come largely as a result of the change in labour law that allowed dispatch agencies to supply teachers to public schools. The agencies were instrumental in bringing Filipinos and other non-native teachers into schools, but at lower salaries and more precarious conditions of employment than were given to ALTs hired under the JET programme or directly by the BoEs. Lori has been fortunate in securing work with a BoE, but Elma's career in Japan has been less auspicious. Elma was able to obtain teaching work normally reserved for 'native speakers' at a time when most Filipinos were excluded from English teaching in Japan. In order to move to Japan with its higher earnings prospects, however, Elma lost the social status the she had in the Philippines as a university lecturer. Moreover, as ever-increasing numbers of Filipinos have entered the English teaching field, the working conditions for Elma have deteriorated as Lori's have improved. Since she lost her *eikaiwa* job, Elma's income is pieced together from various kinds of teaching work.

Norton's notion of identity draws largely on Bourdieu's concept of habitus. Defined as the confluence of our past experience and our present circumstances, both material and ideological, which predisposes us to think and act in specific ways (Bourdieu, 1984, 1990, 1991), Bourdieu's emphasis on 'predisposing' forces and circumstances has led to his social theory being attacked as 'deterministic' (Fabiani, 2016; Jenkins, 1982). Applying the notion of habitus to Lori and Elma, it could be argued that their past experiences before arriving in Japan and since, and the material and ideological circumstances that they have subsequently found themselves in, have predisposed them to ways of thinking about work, and also to ways of thinking about what it means to be an English teacher. Norton's (2013: 45) conceptualisation of identity, by contrast – 'how a person understands his or her relationship to the world, how that relationship is structured across time and space, and how the person understands possibilities for the future' – appears to restore a sense of agency to the individual, and she does this chiefly through the notion of investment. As Claire Kramsch (2013) puts it:

> Norton's notion of investment accentuates the role of human agency and identity: in engaging with the task at hand, in accumulating economic and symbolic capital, in having stakes in the endeavour, and in persevering in that endeavour. (Kramsch, 2013: 195)

This notion of investment is not absent from the narratives of Lori and Elma: it is clear that they have 'invested' in their English teacher identity and they have profited in return, in Elma's case enough to start up a new pre-school in the Philippines, and in Lori's case enough to secure a stable living and higher social status for herself and her children. But as a theoretical concept for understanding identity, the metaphor of investment, with its associations with human capital and emphasis on profit, also obscures some very important aspects of their teaching lives: namely, the emotions of pride and prejudice that are expressed as Filipinos in Japan and the role of the Filipino community. I would like to argue that insights into emotions as a basis of language teacher identity can be gained from recognition theories, and it is to the concept of recognition that I turn now.

Recognition

As I explained in Chapter 2, recognition theories, unlike poststructuralist theories, assume an ontological 'inner core' that can be strengthened by recognition of the qualities of the individual or group and undermined by discrimination or prejudice. In the words of Charles Taylor:

> our identity is partly shaped by recognition or its absence, often by the misrecognition of others, and so a person or group of people can suffer real damage, real distortion, if the people or society around them mirror back to them a confining or demeaning or contemptible picture of

themselves. Nonrecognition or misrecognition can inflict harm, can be a form of oppression, imprisoning someone in a false, distorted, and reduced mode of being. (Taylor, 1994: 25)

Compared to habitus, which represents identity in spatial terms, as the confluence of accumulated experience or capital and social positioning, this view of identity is based on intersubjective recognition, the effects of which are seen in emotions.

In recent years, a number of researchers have taken the view that emotion is crucial to understanding the construction of identity not only of language learners (Benesch, 2012; Miyahara, 2015) but also of teachers (Agudo, 2018; Benesch, 2012, 2017; Said, 2015; Song, 2016; Zemblyas, 2003). Theoretically, emotion researchers have tended to adopt a post-structuralist perspective, which has meant that the focus is on how teacher identity is 'constantly becoming in a context embedded in power relations, ideology, and culture' and 'power is understood as forming the identity and providing the very condition of its trajectory' (Zemblyas, 2003: 213). More specifically in relation to language teacher identity, Sarah Benesch (2012) draws on post-structuralist theorists such as the feminist theorist Sara Ahmed (2004) to argue that emotions emerge not from the individual human psyche but from social contexts and cultural scripts. More recently, Benesch (2017) has deployed concepts of *emotion management*, *emotion work* and *emotion labour* (Hochsschild, 1979) to explore the shifting and overlapping emotions that are evoked when institutional policies and practices clash with a teacher's sense of identity, their professional training and ethics. Juyoung Song (2016), too, adopts a post-structuralist perspective in her study of 'vulnerability' in English language teachers in South Korea. This study showed that feelings of insecurity about their professional competence were evoked in some teachers by returnee students, which hindered their pedagogical and professional transformation; in other teachers, however, openness about their feelings contributed to more engagement by teachers and students and a more transformative experience for both. Song concludes that the emotional experiences of the teachers could be traced back to social and institutional contexts. Both Benesch and Song contend that critical awareness of the social origins of the felt experiences of power and powerlessness opens the way to resistance and empowerment by teachers.

A different theoretical focus, however, is apparent in Motha and Lin's (2014) important article on the concept of *desire*. The authors note that desire connects with various other concepts that have been used to explore identity, including investment and motivation, the romantic desire known as *akogare* (Piller & Takahashi, 2006), commodification of language, radicalised identities, colonialism and communicative language teaching. Motha and Lin, however, take a perspective on desire that aligns more closely with recognition theories. 'Our desires', as they define them, 'are not solely our own but are intersubjectively constituted and shaped by social, historical, political, institutional, and economic contexts' (Motha & Lin, 2014: 331). Seen in this light, the desires or motivations of Lori and Elma have all been mediated through others: Lori abandons her medical studies in the Philippines to come to Japan because of her sister and Elma comes to Japan with her friend, Marie, who has relatives already living in the country. Japan is attractive for them because it is attractive for other Filipinos. As I have mentioned, Lori wants to become an English teacher, not merely because of the economic and social benefits teaching affords but also because other Filipinos desire this occupation too. Although a feeling of desire is necessary to explain teacher's identity and identity formation, however, I would argue that it is not sufficient; mutual recognition is also crucial.

A powerful illustration of this can be seen in Lori's account of her participation in the Hiroshima teaching seminar. At this point, she felt 'afraid to speak or perform in front of a group ... afraid to talk about my classes'. When her American co-participant chides her for seeming to make fun of her during a role play activity, Lori is shocked and angered. As she states in her narrative: 'I realised that you can't teach with that attitude. You can't take yourself so seriously in front of the children'. But although she believes that the American teacher was in the wrong, she is silenced by her anger. Like the other Filipino teachers whom Aurora decided to help by setting up FETJ, Lori does not feel she has the right to speak up in front of 'native speakers'. Even though no one tells the Filipino teachers directly that they are not considered legitimate English teachers, they feel that this is how others regard them. Lori had experienced success as a teacher of kindergarten children, but she felt powerless to retaliate when she received the very public put-down by the American teacher.

A further illustration is served by the account that Elma gives of winning awards as one of the best teachers in her *eikaiwa* school ('*As a Filipino I had to prove myself, I had to be better than other teachers*'). Elma is aware, even at the end of her story when it had become far easier for Filipinos to work as English teachers, that there may still be some stigma against them. For Elma, one of the leading members of FETJ, the feeling that Filipinos need to excel to receive recognition persists ('*Once you show them that you are better than other teachers, they respect you and like you*').

From these examples, we can infer that Filipino teachers find empowerment not by overcoming the social conditions that render them relatively powerlessness, but by receiving recognition for the high degree of professional competence that they are able to bring to their classrooms. Recognition is accorded to Filipino English teachers in various different social domains: in institutions that employ Filipino teachers, and in society at large. Participation in these domains allows Filipinos to show themselves to be worthy of recognition. But access to participation is – or at least until quite recently was – limited. The criticism that I have levelled in this chapter at Norton's concept of investment notwithstanding, the denial of access to participation is the ethical cornerstone on which her theory of language and identity is built. Following the political activist and philosopher Cornell West, Norton asserts the position that

> identity references desire – the desire for recognition, the desire for affiliation, and the desire for security and safety [...] The question 'Who am I?' cannot be understood apart from the question 'What am I allowed to do?'. (Norton, 2013: 48)

In Chapter 4, I take up the subject of identity politics and the role of FETJ in making English teaching in Japan something that Filipinos could be allowed to do.

4 Language Teacher Group Identity

The identity of language teacher groups and the influence of such groups on individual teacher identity is an area that has received relatively scant attention, although two major publications – a special issue of *ELT Journal* edited by Amos Paran (2016) and an anthology of articles edited by Aymen Elsheikh, Christine Coombe and Okon Effiong (2018) – indicate that there is burgeoning interest in this area. In this chapter, the narrative of Sampaguita Salazar, who played a key role in the formation of Filipino English Teacher in Japan (FETJ), provides a backdrop to a discussion of identity as recognition in language teacher associations (LTAs).

I first met Sampaguita, an energetic woman then in her late 50s, at a meeting of FETJ at which two proposals were put forward concerning new directions for the group. One was a venture capital scheme in which FETJ teachers would qualify for a loan to set up English pre-schools with day care, the other a new certificated teaching English as a second language (TESOL) course for Filipino teachers for which some internationally known TESOL teachers had already stated an interest in joining as special lecturers. Both proposals involved money, and ultimately both were rejected. The proposals came at a point in time when FETJ was changing direction – away from the social activism that had characterised its activities in the previous five-year period. The people who were now most influential in the organisation, including Sampaguita, resisted the enhanced role of social activism inherent in the venture capital proposal, but they also resisted the commercial identity that characterised the TESOL course proposal.

The following narrative was recorded in summer 2015, a few years after that meeting. Aurora had invited me to a Saturday morning 'English and Martial Arts' event organised by FETJ. Sampaguita left the event at two points during the proceedings, and we sat in the corridor near a power socket so that I could keep my computer plugged in as I recorded her story. One thing that is not captured in the narrative, but that I would like you to imagine as you read, is the laughter that punctuates Sampaguita's telling of her story.

Sampaguita's Story

I came in the late part of 2006. My grandfather was Japanese, we're sansei [third-generation Japanese]. *A group of Japanese businessmen came to us, saying they were an NPO and they could get us a visa for Japan. We're like ants, we said OK, we'll go to Japan and we all came, apart from two who had gone to live in the States. But some went back, so it's just four of us here now. And all of us are teachers.*

Life in the Philippines before I came to Japan? Well, not to brag, but I held a very nice position. I worked for Avon where I was in charge of quality control of all non-cosmetic products. The job involved a lot of traveling, so for 11 years of my life I was traveling to China, Hong Kong, America. I started in Avon as the secretary to the Regional Managing Director of Avon Philippines, then when the regional offices closed I got moved to the Purchasing Department. I'm not an engineer, but my husband is, and he was always at my back asking questions: 'What is this? What are the specifications for that?' So when I gave a presentation for Avon, they were, 'Wow, perfect!' My husband had a very good job as well, as an engineer designing buildings and machines. And then we came to Japan, and we were peeling pineapples! We didn't know what the life would be like. My husband is into technical work and we thought, people in Japan need technical workers, he can get a better job there. And at that time, Avon offered a handsome delayering package, 5 million pesos tax free, so I got the visa, and I said to my husband, we've got this money, why not try in Japan?

So we arrived and were taken to my sister's place – she had arrived a few months earlier. You know, in the Philippines we have the idea that everywhere else is like America. I had traveled, but I'd never been to Japan. But at the same time I was really proud of Japan, because of my grandfather. So when I came, I was really disgusted to see such small houses, such poor conditions, and I wanted to tell my husband, 'Don't come'. But the recruiter had already told my husband that I was missing him and he should come. All my family members had handed over their passports and visa so they were all tied up with these Japanese recruiters. I refused to hand over mine – I know my rights. And I told them that I had paid them for all their service back in the Philippines. I had given them two cheques which had cleared, so there was proof of payment. But we really had a terrible fight. And then when my husband came, they wanted to pick him up at the airport but I said, 'No, I will go. Don't come with me'. I knew they would try to take his visa and passport otherwise. But after that, I went to the Ministry of Labour to complain about the recruiters and they said they would protect us until City Hall helped us to find another job. The recruiters promised us different work, but that was just promises.

Instead, I had the opportunity to teach English in a school. It was for one day only. But the school featured me in their website as the best teacher they'd ever had. This was my first day! So I thought, OK, so I can teach. After that I applied to hakengaishas [dispatch agencies] and I was assigned to work in another school. At the end of the contract, all the teachers applauded me and the principal gave me a framed photograph. Wow! So I carried on teaching short-term jobs like this from January to March, and then I was employed on a regular annual contract. But my husband was still stuck peeling vegetables. I knew he was not happy. I was already stable in a teaching career. In the Philippines, we had property: two big mansions. We lost one because we couldn't keep up the payments but we kept making the payments for the other. Then he was hired in the Philippines. But we applied for permanent visa. So he came here, went to the immigration office to get the visa and went straight home. But he has to come back every year.

So now I enjoy my life in Japan. I have two grown-up children who are already working. My second son was a speech champion in high school for three years in a row. He's now in sales in realty and we bought our next property, a bungalow, through him – we gave him the first commission. Now my husband is a vice president of Robinsons. I'm happy with the job here now. We thought maybe this is a good training for our children. We had never been apart not even for a day. We shall not be here forever, so maybe this is a kind of practice for the future. We become stronger and independent.

My family is all in teaching or connected with education. My father was a school principal, one of my sisters was secretary in a graduate school. I was the only one in business. So my younger sister was my coach in the first months. She gave me materials, she said you have to do this and this. Now she has her own school and my other sister has her own school.

I don't know Japanese, so I just use my charm. They all laugh at me. So when I say 'yoroshiku onegaishimasu' [I beg your indulgence], they all laugh and find me cute. I say 'I'm sorry I can't speak Japanese', and they say 'Don't worry, we will help you'. And over lunch I ask questions about the food, like 'kore nan desuka? Kore ninjin desuka?' ['What is this? Is this a carrot?'] So I volunteer to do all the jobs like cleaning the sink and even cleaning the toilet, and that impresses them. And they say, 'The children are really looking forward to English class every time'. That isn't the way for every teacher. I have an innate passion as a teacher. Actually, I always wanted to be a teacher. We were very poor and that's why I went to secretarial school, I could get a good salary quite quickly. So I did a two-year course and then continued school at night until I got a bachelors. So it wasn't until I came to Japan that I discovered I was a teacher. This is where I found my career.

My very first experience in junior high school, I saw some of the students sleeping in my class, and I was shocked, I felt maybe I do something wrong. I asked the teacher and she said, 'Don't worry, it's normal'. But

I was depressed, I didn't want to have students sleeping. So I went up to these sleepy students and tried to talk to them and tried to understand where they were coming from. Inside I was crying for them, so I tried to give them some special attention, some personal contact.

So now I've taught all levels of students. I was teaching in the Kaisen Foreign and International Office, and they were happy with me because I was a teacher. When my mother came, they made a big fuss of her and interviewed her. Saitama [Prefecture Board of Education] only allows us to work for five hours, so I had to find other work elsewhere. So by word of mouth, I started collecting private students. And the money I can get from these classes has gone up and up.

At first, I was still struggling and I really wanted to know more. I heard about an English workshop, so I went along and I learned a lot from Kathleen Kampa. And then I heard about an FETJ workshop but at that time it was bara bara *[disorganised]. I went along in the afternoon, and it was already over in the morning. 'Next week we have another one', so when I came, it was Armando who was facilitating, and it was the first time he did it, and he wasn't really good then. And there was one rule that I questioned. Aurora was shocked, she said 'It's the first time anyone has questioned my class'. So then I said, 'Instead of criticising, why don't I help?'. So speaking on the phone with Aurora after that, she said 'Why don't you come and teach a workshop?'. So that was awesome. And then I suggested that it have more structure. It can't be just a mother–daughter relationship, you have to have rules. So that's how the chapters were formed. And that is when Aurora and I started having disagreements. All the time, I don't know that Aurora is approving something. I don't mind if she wants to stay in control, but if she decides something, then I have to know. It took us two and a half years to get to know each other in terms of management. So what I do now, if I know she has decided, my role is to support her. All of the problems, I try to sort them out. Like the chapters, Saitama started to get really big, and so rather than have too many people in one chapter, we decided to form a new chapter, Saitama 2.*

So on the executive board we have Katrina on the website, Armando in charge of external affairs because of his nihongo [Japanese language], May in treasury. With the young people coming up, in other regions we have strong leaders, it's a question of dedication. If all of us go, FETJ will go on. We have a strong structure. And it's becoming more global: FETJ-Global. This is like Avon – the name of the company is FETJ, but we have affiliates in different countries. I know management, corporate set-up, I did that for 21 years. So I know what it is, I know what I'm talking about.

Arriving in Japan some 20 years later than Elma, Sampaguita's story of success is strikingly different from the narratives in Chapter 3. The anecdote about how she came to Japan with which she begins her narrative is an instance not just of discrimination but of fraudulent inducement and forced labour. Sampaguita blames herself and her family for being seduced by the Japanese businessmen who recruited them. As *sansei* with a legal right to employment in Japan, they did not suspect that they would be duped in this way ('*We are like ants*'). The point of the anecdote, however, is that she was able to outsmart the recruiters, refusing to give them her passport or let them take her husband's, and refusing to give them more money, which they presumably demanded after she arrived in Japan. Apart from the attempted violation of her rights by these recruitment agents, however, Sampaguita does not experience or sense any discrimination against her as a Filipino in Japan. The Japanese authorities come to her aid when she complains about the recruitment agents who brought her to Japan, and provide her with teaching work that proves to be the start of her new career. The Japanese teachers she works with think she is 'cute' and appreciate her willingness to help. Indeed, rather than any negative attitude towards her, it is Sampaguita who at times looks down on the Japanese. Proud of her Japanese heritage as *sansei*, Sampaguita had assumed that Japan would be as affluent in appearance as the United States, and so she feels 'disgust' at the 'small houses and poor conditions' that she encounters when she first arrives.

It is perhaps surprising that Sampaguita decides to stay on in Japan after her traumatic experience with the Japanese recruiters and when she discovers that Japan was not as she had imagined it would be. The phrase 'not to brag but...' implies the opposite: that her life and career with a multinational company in the Philippines were indeed something to brag about. But perhaps she had intended to become an English teacher in Japan even before she left her job at Avon. Other members of her family were teachers, and she claims teaching was something she always wanted to do. In Japan, she is able to fulfil her dream of becoming a teacher, a role for which she feels she has 'an innate passion'. For Sampaguita, a teacher identity comes naturally and quickly, rather than developing over a long period of time.

Sampaguita's experience of teaching has been positive from the very start. It was the Japanese authorities that gave her a first taste: a day's teaching in a school, at the end of which she was showered with praise and presents. After three months of short-term teaching jobs, she was able to secure a regular teaching position as an assistant language teacher (ALT). In fact, she was the last member of her family to become a teacher and it was her family members who helped her with advice and materials in the first months of teaching. Thereafter, like Lori, she attended teacher training events in order to develop her skills and it was through doing this that she first came across FETJ.

Prejudice and pride are reflected in a singular way also in Sampaguita's recounting of her experiences in the schools. Unable to speak much Japanese, she 'wins over' the Japanese teachers with her charm, but also, clearly, with her efforts to learn Japanese. She also impresses teachers by her willingness to do things, such as cleaning toilets, which she implies other foreign teachers might balk at. Sampaguita does not appear to feel entitled to any special rights as a foreigner or foreign teacher. She does, however, feel a responsibility as a teacher to try to reach all her students, and does not accept the Japanese teacher's explanation that it is normal for students to sleep through the English class. There is no hint that prejudice is directed at her. But in the expression of her feelings about the sleeping students (*'Inside I was crying for them, so I tried to give them some special attention, some personal contact'*), it could be argued that she believes the students are discriminated against because they are ignored by the Japanese teacher, deprived of any personal contact.

Sampaguita's story highlights occasions when her knowledge and skills are recognised: by the schools where she works, by the Kaisen Foreign and International Office, by the increasing number of private students who add to her income and by FETJ. Recognition by others goes hand in hand with Sampaguita's self-confidence. Although relatively new to teaching, she has the confidence to speak up and challenge one of Aurora's 'rules' and is then invited by Aurora to teach a workshop. Sampaguita has strong views on how to run an organisation (*'I know management, corporate set-up, I did that for 21 years. So I know what it is, I know what I'm talking about'*). Her contribution to the group has been to help change it from a 'mother–daughter' relationship, which typified Aurora's relationship with members previously, to a 'corporate' entity, a strong structure that can continue even after individual members have moved on.

But it is also clear that her decisions and actions do not pass uncontested. Sampaguita laughs when she says that she and Aurora started arguing after the chapters were formed; my impression of their relationship was that they are close friends. Nevertheless, although she does not say so directly, it can be inferred that there was a power struggle between the two women, each of whom appear to imagine FETJ in quite different ways: Sampaguita sees it as an organisation based on corporate structures and principles, while Aurora imagines a far looser entity that she can influence and direct as she sees fit. Sampaguita notes that it took more than two and a half years for them to get to know each other in terms of management. The outcome appears to be a compromise: Aurora remains 'in control', but Sampaguita wants to know about her decisions so that she (and the organisation) can support her.

The 'disagreement' that Sampaguita alludes to is a struggle over the evolving identity of FETJ: from a 'mother and daughter' relationship between Aurora and the women she helps and a large and expanding organisation based on rules and regulations. However, this was not the only struggle in the formation of FETJ's identity. In the following section, I give an account of these based on my observations and conversations with FETJ members, as well as on what we learn about the origin and evolution of the group in the narratives of Aurora and Lori.

FETJ's Identity Formation

The initial formation of the group that became FETJ could be defined as social activism, although Aurora called it a 'study group' to enable Filipinos to practice and talk about the teaching methods and materials that they were shown at English Teachers in Japan (ETJ) expos. But the organisation that I came to know nearly 10 years later seemed to me to be clearly dedicated to the enhancement of Filipino identity in Japan through English teaching. An important role in this development is played by another group that is mentioned in Lori's narrative. Lori relates how she ran teacher training workshops for Filipino women together with a missionary friend and this enterprise had merged with FETJ for a period in 2005. The friend she is referring to is Cesar Santoyo, a lay missionary and social activist, who arrived in Japan in 2001 on a 'sent mission' by the United Churches of Christ Philippines (UCCP) as the director of the Centre for Filipino Families in Japan (CFFJ). In an ethnographic study of this organisation, Docot (2009) reports on how the purpose of the mission was primarily ideological, aimed at countering a neocolonial policy of forced migration of Filipino women with one of migrant support and the building of a multicultural Japan. More than simple protection of Filipino women, many of whom became victims of domestic abuse, or, like Lori, ended up as single mothers in Japan, the CFFJ has prioritised the empowerment of Filipino women as economic agents.

A first initiative of CFFJ was the formation of a group called Community of Home-based English Teachers (CHOBET), and it was this group that organised the workshops in which Lori started her activity as a teacher trainer. The pro-Filipino, multiculturalist ideology espoused by CHOBET, as well as by subsequent English teaching groups that sprang up, including FETJ, is undoubtedly a factor in motivating women in similar situations to become teachers. The focus of CHOBET was on home-based teaching, in other words, on teaching as a business, just as we saw in Lori's narrative. In 2005, when Aurora left Japan to return to the Philippines to embark on a master's degree, Lori and Cesar merged the two organisations, CHOBET and FETJ.

In his work as a social activist advocating for Filipino migrants in Japan, Santoyo acknowledges that 'you cannot separate economics from politics' (cited in Docot, 2009). Empowering Filipinos in Japan means giving them the means to economic independence and growth, but this is also a political endeavour. This marriage of social justice with economics and politics resonates with the recent work of feminist critical theorist Nancy Fraser. In an extended debate, Fraser argues against Honneth's position that the struggle for recognition is primary and the distribution of wealth secondary, and proposes instead a dual perspective in which social recognition and economic redistribution are seen as two equal but separate categories both of which are 'co-fundamentally and mutually irreducible dimensions of justice' (Fraser & Honneth, 2003: 3). In more recent work, Fraser (2013: 193) argues that in a world where the nation-state is losing its relevance, social justice needs to be re-envisaged in global terms to incorporate 'the political dimension of representation, alongside the economic dimension of distribution and the cultural dimension of recognition'. As an activist, thus, it is not enough to train Filipino women who came to Japan as entertainers to become English language teachers; it is also necessary to provide them with economic capital to set up new schools, and access to other institutions that can secure them fruitful and stable employment.

Indeed, venture capital to set up small schools was what Santoyo was proposing at the meeting I described at the start of this chapter. But his was not the only proposal. At the same meeting, another Filipino, Lynn Suico, proposed setting up a TESOL diploma course to be taught by recognised experts in the field. As we saw in Lori's narrative, such courses command significant fees from participants, and after the meeting I was party to conversations in which the proposer was criticised for apparently seeking to exploit Filipinos for profit. Both the venture capital scheme and the TESOL diploma proposal were rejected at this time, and FETJ consolidated its identity as a provider of training and support for new teachers. Aurora appeared to be the primary decision-maker, with Sampaguita also playing a key role.

A number of important events occurred as part of this process of consolidation. A Filipino businessman and English language teacher was invited to become president of FETJ, with Aurora apparently stepping sideways into an honorary role as chairman and founder, as well as chief trainer. The organisation was registered with the Philippines Embassy as a legal corporate entity. A mission statement and logo were created and a constitution drawn up, prescribing roles for officers of the organisation in the national executive committee and in local chapters. It was established that an annual fee of 1000 yen would be levied on members (a fee that has since been raised to 2000 yen), and the workshops themselves became more formalised. A teaching guidelines handbook was created for use in the Teaching Guidelines Seminar for pre-service teachers particularly of young learners and elementary schools. A range of courses was established: the basic teaching guidelines, advanced teacher training (for pre- and in-service teachers in junior high schools) and training of trainers, as well as workshops on grammar, pronunciation, business English and job-seeking preparation. Although the members of local chapters were encouraged to practice the techniques and activities that were taught in the seminars and to propose variations and improvements, the basic teaching remained the preserve of a small group of appointed trainers and Aurora. Subsequently, disputes over this type of control led to occasional ructions between the executive board and local chapters.

The two most influential actors, apart from Aurora, were Glen, the new president, and Sampaguita, and it is their efforts that led to the corporatisation of FETJ. However, the need for a clearer and stronger structure can also be explained by factors such as, most notably, the rapid expansion of the organisation. Dispatch agencies had been employing Filipino teachers from the early 2000s, but from 2010, local boards of education in the Kanto area around Tokyo also started hiring Filipinos directly, and so more Filipinos were attracted by the career opportunities that English teaching presented. In its homepage, FETJ started describing itself as 'an association of Filipino English teachers in Japan which provides support to its members by facilitating regular education through trainings, continuous communication, and assistance in job placements'. The website goes on to state that 'the organization aims to serve as bridge between members and other related institutions including Japanese Board of Education (sic), serving as a liaison'. Although it maintained a website linked to the much larger network, ETJ, FETJ's main medium of communication with its members from this time was through Facebook, which started to become ubiquitous among Filipinos. Thus, not only social changes, but also changes in communication technology influenced the developing identity of the organisation and the need for a different kind of structure.

Having described some of the dynamics that were present in the formation of FETJ, I turn now to consider its identity and role in light of the small body of research that is concerned with LTAs. In particular, I want to discuss the question of how we might define LTAs and whether or not this is an identity that applies to FETJ.

Language Teacher Associations

As mentioned, until recently there has been an 'alarming paucity' of research into LTAs (Aubrey & Coombe, 2010: para. 10). A landmark study in the area is Lamb's (2012) survey of the member associations of the International Federation of LTAs, which showed that these organisations, most of them based in Europe, viewed their identity and their role as akin to professional associations in occupations other than language teaching. Based on the findings of the survey, Lamb (2012: 295) highlights this association with professionalism in his definition of LTAs as 'networks of professionals, run by and for professionals, focused mainly on support for members, with knowledge exchange and development as well as representation of members' views as their defining functions'.

Nevertheless, the LTAs in Lamb's survey also differed in quite significant ways from the traditional characterisations of professional associations in occupations such as nursing and accountancy. A classic definition of professional associations (Kloss, 1999) characterises them as composed of two key features: firstly, professional associations have both external functions (advocacy) and internal functions (towards members); and secondly, with regard to their internal orientation, they have a normative function in setting standards of practice. In Lamb's survey, the International Federation of LTAs claimed that they served external functions of advocacy, as well as internal functions of supporting the professional development needs of their members. The survey also found that members regarded the associations as empowering spaces for professional networking. However, it did not reveal any emphasis on the normative function that is assumed in classic definitions of professional associations.

Inspired by Lamb's study, Masuko Miyahara and I conducted a survey of four major LTAs in Japan (Stewart & Miyahara, 2016) and we found four quite different kinds of organisation. In other words, the LTAs were remarkably diverse. We also drew on a historical overview of LTAs in Japan by Koike (2013), which suggested that the changing social context, including successive reforms in English education, may have been a factor in creating this diversity. Following on from this, Masuko and I looked to Foucault's (1980) concept of *power/knowledge* to argue that the various kinds of LTAs could be characterised according to whether they were producers of knowledge or disseminators of knowledge. In other words, production of knowledge would include advocacy of theory and practice through consultation and publication, while dissemination would include teacher training and selling or promoting books and materials. Only one of the LTAs that we surveyed – the Japan Association of College English Teachers (JACET) – claimed to have an advocacy role, through its consultation with MEXT. Knowledge production was not highlighted as a major feature of any of these LTAs.

FETJ was not one of the LTAs included in our survey, but in many ways it adheres more closely to the classic definition of a professional organisation than do the larger LTAs that we chose for our LTA study. Towards its members, FETJ has a strongly normative function in setting standards of practice for teaching. These practices are codified in the teaching guidelines handbook that Aurora wrote and conformity is maintained by confining the role of teacher trainer to a small and close-knit team. Participants of the training seminars are assessed on their uptake of the teaching principles and on their suitability for work as teachers. More interestingly, FETJ plays the role of advocate, not only of a method of teaching, but also of the participants of the seminars. Participants who complete the seminars are awarded certificates that could help them gain work, for example with dispatch companies. Outstanding participants are selected for personal recommendation to local boards of education.

In the *Encyclopedia of Applied Linguistics*, Ehlers-Savala (2012) states that 'advocacy in language teaching refers to the act of positively advancing the public and political realities connected to issues in language and language teaching' and that 'an advocate in language teaching is someone who espouses and argues for one or more issues in language teaching hoping to positively influence its outcome for the common good'. This use of advocacy points primarily to the recommendation of causes or policy. However, in the case of FETJ, the function of advocacy is evident in a social justice sense of the protection and promotion of the rights of certain groups of people. The use of advocacy in this sense can be seen in Lia Kamhi-Stein's (2016) study of the non-native English-speaking professionals' movement within the TESOL International Association. Rather than a language teaching association, Kamhi-Stein calls it a 'movement', although she describes how it was initially termed an interest group and later a caucus within the larger organisation. Advocacy of non-native English teachers is also prominent in a website 'campaign' called TEFL Equity Advocates and Academy, which was founded by Marek Kiczkowiak in 2014.

However, FETJ is more than a movement or a campaign advocating for the rights of Filipinos to work as English teachers. On the homepage of its website, FETJ defines itself as 'an association of Filipino English teachers in Japan which provides support to its members by facilitating regular education through trainings, continuous communication, and assistance in job placements'. As we have seen, the role and identity of FETJ has changed over time as a result of changes in its leadership and rapid growth in its membership. Sampaguita's main contribution has been to strengthen the organisation by giving it a corporate-style structure that will ensure its continuity even if individual leaders are no longer with the organisation.

Like other LTAs (Uludag, 2018), FETJ has adopted a management structure to enable it to deal with its growth and spread, as well as to bring it into line with other associations. Another reason for this type of management structure was its registration as a legal entity. In the initial discussions regarding the direction of FETJ, the lucrative TESOL courses were rejected in favour of continuing the basic training for new teachers. Nonetheless, FETJ does collect membership fees, as well as fees for its teacher training courses, and it pays for its trainers' travel expenses, all of which requires responsible money management by a treasurer. Other LTAs around the world are legal corporate entities, but this may take different forms. The Japan Association of Language Teaching, for example, is a non-profit organisation (NPO) registered in Japan. The International Association of Teachers of English as a Foreign Language (IATEFL) in the UK is a registered charity. These legal identities define the organisation's relationship with the state of the country in which they are located (e.g. whether they pay taxes or not) and the registration of an organisation, or the act of incorporation, fixes the organisation's purpose.

Although in this respect, FETJ is no different from other large LTAs, it raises questions regarding how we might define its identity. Although Lamb (2012: 295) maintained that LTAs are 'networks of professionals, run by professionals', he refrained from defining them as 'professional associations'. The question of whether or not language teaching is a 'profession' at all has been subject to some debate in the past (Johnston, 1997; MacPherson *et al.*, 2005), and I will return to this question of professional identity for a more detailed discussion in Chapter 5. Certainly, in its mission statement, FETJ does not claim to be a 'professional association', defining itself merely as 'an association of Filipino English teachers in Japan'. But in its teaching activities, the organisation does serve a normative function, since its seminars are confined to a tested format and materials. The participants who take these seminars are not professionals yet, but they hope to become professional teachers.

If not a professional association, what other identities could be applied to FETJ? I observed that FETJ was registered with the Embassy of the Philippines as a legal corporate entity, and through Sampaguita's narrative it is evident that she regards it as an entrepreneurial venture, about which she has strong opinions. As a former executive, Sampaguita has had experience of 'management, corporate set-up'. She is thus critical when practices do not meet the standards she expected from her career in Avon. The first FETJ meeting that she tries to attend does not take place at the time that was advertised; the second is led by someone who she implies was not competent in conducting the event. Similarly, her corporate expertise gives her clear views on how to maintain control, for example, by ruling that local chapters should be kept small and when they grow too big, to divide them into smaller groups. Most of all, Sampaguita sees FETJ like Avon, as a high-quality 'brand' that can be marketed across Japan and abroad. Ironically, the 'Global' suffix that Sampaguita applies to FETJ relates to the seminars that Aurora and others have conducted in the Philippines. Thus, Filipino English Teacher in Japan is a brand that is exported to the Philippines.

The concept of a brand is usually associated with marketisation, and it has been discussed in highly critical terms as such, for example by Block (2018) with regard to self-definition and self-promotion in neoliberal ideology, and by Lorente (2017) with regard to the promotion of Filipinos as overseas workers. In the following section, I argue that the notion of 'brand' is not merely entrepreneurial self-marketisation, but can also be explained in terms of the identity-as-recognition model that I have discussed in previous chapters.

Recognition: Logos and Awards

A key moment in the consolidation of FETJ's identity was the creation of its logo, designed using the colours of the national flag of the Philippines, and bearing the words, 'Filipino Teachers in Japan: Friendship, Unity, Excellence'. The logo appears on large banners hung in the rooms and halls where FETJ seminars, workshops and events take place. It also appears on all posters and flyers that are created to advertise such events and it is displayed on its website. Such branding is not merely for the purposes of identification, it is also for promoting recognition of FETJ among potential participants, its customers or consumers in entrepreneurial terms, and among the potential employers of those participants. The logo also serves an internal function, that of instilling pride in its members as 'Filipino English teachers'.

Pride and recognition go beyond symbols of identity such as the logo. Tokens of recognition are also seen in the certificates that are signed by Aurora, and which for a while I also signed; these are printed on stiff card bearing the FETJ logo. As I have mentioned, these certificates are used by participants as evidence of some kind of qualification and are accepted as such by dispatch companies familiar with FETJ and its activities. Tokens of recognition, such as framed awards, are also given to members of the executive as signs of appreciation for the service that they render to the organisation. Autoethnographic accounts of leadership roles in LTAs by Serrano and Schrader (2018) and Dickey (2018) have highlighted the importance of extending this kind of recognition for the well-being of the organisation and to encourage the continuing voluntary efforts of its active members. Named roles or titles are an important feature of this kind of recognition, and in the case of FETJ, the conferring of such roles and titles, such as treasurer or membership officer, is performed at an annual swearing-in ceremony officiated by a high-ranking officer from the Embassy of the Philippines. This level of ceremony is perhaps unusual compared with other LTAs, although it may not be unprecedented among other social groups that many Filipinos belong to in Japan.

Recognition is thus oriented both outwards (profit) and inwards (pride). Tokens of identity, such as the logo for the organisation as a whole, or the certificates awarded to successful participants of the training seminars, serve to market the FETJ brand. As such, this outward direction can be said to be 'profit oriented' since the people who take the courses raise their chances of gaining teaching employment; their value as 'human capital' is enhanced. Moreover, this enhanced value comes not merely from the experience and knowledge that is gained from the training courses, but also – indeed, more so – from the FETJ name. Inward recognition can include the recognition of individuals for their service and achievements on behalf of the group, as well as the celebration of a shared culture.

The tropes of 'pride' and 'profit' have been examined and discussed in depth in relation to language in the anthology edited by Alexandre Duchêne and Monica Heller (2012), with pride referring to cultural heritage that is indexed by the language, and profit referring to the economic advantage that proficiency in a language is supposed to confer. As Heller and Duchêne (2012) observe, pride and profit are not separate or opposite, but are intertwined. With regard to language teacher identity, pride and profit are both implicated in the role of FETJ; however, as I showed in the negotiations on the organisation's future, it is the participants who stand to profit by gaining access to teaching work, and not the organisation or the people who run it. FETJ's corporate identity and symbols draw on entrepreneurial discourses, but the mission of the organisation is the enhancement – both social and economic – of its (largely) Filipino members.

In this chapter, I have described what I observed of the process of identity formation of FETJ and I have discussed how we might define this organisation. FETJ has taken a middle course between two extremes: one focusing solely on the enhancement of Filipino status in Japan, which was represented and promoted by Cesar Santoyo, and another as a purveyor of accredited TESOL courses that would have yielded considerable profit. The institutionalisation of the group, the fixing of its management structure, purpose and brand imply an entrepreneurial, corporate identity, and this is certainly Sampaguita's view. As such, it is significantly different from LTAs that claim (or aspire) to be professional associations, thereby implying that their members are already professional teachers. In Chapter 5, I consider the influence of FETJ on three of the younger teachers and rising stars in the group.

5 Careers, Work, Morality

More than 20 years ago, Bill Johnston (1997) asked the question 'Do EFL teachers have careers?' and this is a question that I would like to consider anew in the case of Filipino teachers in Japan. From interviewing English teachers in Poland during a period of dramatic political and economic change, Johnston found that the notion of a stable or unitary career or professional identity did not capture how these teachers talked about their lives. Working in temporary or marginal positions in schools, many teachers made ends meet, or found personal fulfilment by working in other jobs, not necessarily teaching. Subsequently, Johnston (1999) described expatriate English teachers as 'postmodern paladins', drawing a parallel between English teachers working abroad and the noble 'knights errant' of Arthurian legend. Chivalric nobility, in Johnston's metaphor, is reflected in teachers' 'wish to educate' (Johnston, 1999: 259) and in 'a moral duty toward students' (Johnston, 1999: 265). As these two articles suggest, language teaching as work can be conceptualised in very different ways. Language teaching can simply be regarded as a means of making a living, one's 'bread and butter', as Lori called it. It can also be seen as a social practice in which one develops expertise and, perhaps, though not necessarily, enhanced social status. Finally, teaching is an occupation that would seem to be intrinsically moral, as we can see from Johnston's paladin-teachers, but this can present problems in the intercultural classroom. How are these different aspects of work reflected in the narratives of Filipino teachers? In particular, how can an understanding of language teaching as work be enhanced by the concept of identity as recognition?

In the following sections, I present the stories of three younger teachers, Anna Marie Togasaki, Shin Hirata and Katrina Harada, all of whom became English teachers in Japan through Filipino English Teacher in Japan (FETJ). The three teachers are among the 'stars' of the group, rising quickly in their new teaching careers, and remaining actively involved in FETJ. As you read their stories, you may notice how recognition is a stimulus to the formation of their language teacher identity and how this differs from the experiences related by the previous narrators, in particular, Lori and Elma. You may also notice how inscribed identities of ethnicity, gender and sexuality all contribute not only to the sense of agency that is conveyed – what they feel they *can* do – but also to their sense of morality – what they feel they *should* do.

I begin with Anna Marie's narrative. Although I had met her at FETJ social events previously, it was at the martial arts events where I interviewed Sampaguita that I finally had the chance to sit down with her and listen to her story.

Anna Marie's Story

When I came here first, I can't speak Japanese, I can't read or write, I was a real beginner, in Japanese culture and everything. My sister lives here, and ever since high school she stayed here for a very long time and she never came back for five years and I missed her a lot. I came here to meet her and be with her and that's when I met my husband. We had a long-distant relationship after I went back, and then we decided to get married in the Philippines. So the second time I came to Japan was with my husband. I was only 23 when we got married. When I came here I had to study Japanese to do my job as a wife and a mom. It was hard work, it was the hardest period. First I tried to do it by myself, but after that I decided to study. I was a single mum and my husband was a divorced dad. So when I came here I suddenly had two Japanese daughters. She was only in grade school and I had to attend meetings and help her. So I had to give a lot of effort to not just the language but everything, the food, the cooking. So that was a big challenge, but I survived!

My course was a bachelor's of science in business administration, majoring in computer science. At that time, I realized that wasn't my thing. When I was choosing my course, I was choosing not on what my skills were, what I really wanted to do. I just went along with my friends so we could hang out. I wasn't that focused then. I graduated and worked as a salesperson, customer relations staff for a clothing company. I already had my baby then. I was never a teacher in the Philippines. But ever since grade school, English was my favourite subject, and I always excelled in English through school. It comes naturally to me even if I don't study hard. When the teacher comes in, I'm focused and enjoying. Spelling bees, essay writing, speech contests, I loved it all. I hated mathematics – you should see my grades. When I was very young, I loved watching TV programs, cartoons in English. Nobody told me to study. It's in me, it's in my heart. I had a passion to be the best at English.

When I came here, I didn't have any friends, I didn't know anybody. I was lonely, I didn't know how to make friends, I didn't know anything. I went to church one day and saw a lot of Filipinos there. There were Filipino foods being sold, Filipino newspapers, magazines, I felt overwhelmed, I was so happy, and ever since I go to church. That changed everything. I overcame my homesickness. Still, I didn't know I could teach. But ever since then, I wanted to teach. I'm not interested in teaching adults, just kids.

I worked first as a waitress. It was 10 years ago, I was working at Outback American restaurant as an English-speaking hostess. And there Alexia became my best friend. She never told me that her mom was a teacher and I didn't tell her I wanted to teach. I thought that only native speakers could teach in Japan. It was my image, I never met any Asian or any Filipino that was a teacher at that time. Then, after Alexis got married she told me about FETJ and her mom. She told me very casually, 'My mom is having this event, are you free, why don't you check it out?'

The first time I attended an FETJ seminar, it was the teaching guidelines seminar and Ma'am Aurora was leading it. There were lots of Filipinos learning about teaching. I was surprised and said why didn't I know about this ages ago? Oh my god, I wish I had known! I was really happy and I had fun. I learned about things from her and listened to her stories. Starting from that day, I devoted myself as an active member of FETJ. I focused first on learning, on teaching right away. I know my English is OK, but I need the skills on how to teach the language. It's not just being able to speak, it's how to teach. Those techniques, those methods, what is best for kids. Ma'am Aurora did a lot of personal coaching for me. She believed in me, and I was thankful. I still am, I'm a very loyal member of FETJ.

That was more than six or seven years ago. I wasn't able to teach then because I got pregnant, and my husband didn't want me to work pregnant or with a baby. I didn't want to waste that time so I took the opportunity to learn many things through FETJ. I learned about Oxford [University Press], about FETJ, about TESOL, I took a TESOL test, I did a lot of workshops. Then when my daughter started kindergarten, that's when I began teaching. YMCA was my first job. I began teaching kindergarten kids at YMCA and then I started my own little home-based job. The moms asked me to teach their kids, they don't have so much money to pay ECC so they asked me if I can do it at a low price. I did it not for money but as a hobby, as my passion. The mommies always say thanks to me, but actually, I want to thank them because I got to practice all those things I learned at FETJ. At YMCA I had to follow the rules, so this was a chance for me to experiment. It was a big learning experience. I was able to enhance my own teaching skills.

Then when my daughter became second year of kindergarten, I looked for jobs with more hours. Gregg International School has a branch in Jiyugaoka. I just applied, called, and they set me up for an interview and for a demo and a written test, and they called me back, and now it's my third year there. Most of the students are from other countries, and Japanese. I teach not only English, but a little bit of science, math, PE. I'm not an English teacher, I'm a schoolteacher. I teach kindergarten and I'm an adviser for elementary first- and second-year returnees. I teach at Gregg every day, from 8:45 to 2:45. I am really enjoying my job. I love the kids. I work with Japanese co-teachers. Last Friday was our graduation day. Our school year starts September. It was a nice ceremony and I cried. You know, International School is very expensive. Most of our students are sons and daughters of TV personalities. If you watch baseball, Mr Wada, his daughter is at our school. Some parents are ex-models, ex-actresses. One of my students is the son of a popular singer. It's fun working there, the atmosphere is fun. I want to stay. But I'm getting busier and busier.

My job is getting busier every year. They're giving me a lot of work to do. It's OK with me, because I like what I'm doing. I feel happy that they trust me and give me more responsibilities, but my husband wants me to cut down. Either cut this or this. At FETJ also we are very busy, especially with IIEE, an English language school that FETJ is thinking of starting from September. We aren't sure if it's going to be a success or not. We launch it in September. So I'm the coordinator for the Tokyo branch. We have a venue now and I will be the head teacher there. So I'll be working at Gregg, IIEE and FETJ – all three things are busy. So my husband wants me to choose. I don't want to give up any – I'm showing him that I can do my best as a mom and as a wife while keeping all these jobs. I'm so lucky. I'm able to do what I want to do as a career and earn good money from it. I'm doing it because it's my passion. Even if I get so tired, I always feel it's fulfilling and rewarding. That's one of the reasons why I cannot leave FETJ. I will always be grateful.

My worst moment is working with teachers who are not devoted, not passionate, not sincere in what they are doing. It sucks. I hate working with people like that. I'm a really devoted teacher and I'm always willing to learn while I work. One of the things I learned from Aurora is that teaching is continuous learning, lifelong learning. It's true. I've seen teachers who are native English speakers and just not sincere with the kids. I've seen teachers treat the kids badly, saying inappropriate things to the kids. It makes me mad. I never realized there are teachers like that. These are little kids. I have kids too. I have a kid in kindergarten. I felt a bit scared for my kid, that she might be exposed to that kind of teacher. When I was in kindergarten in the Philippines, all the teachers were very friendly. If you're a little kids' teacher, you have to be like that.

The best teaching moments? So many. Actually, every day is like the best teaching moment. I'm always excited to go to work, to plan what we're going to do for the day. After my work is also one of the best moments. It's rewarding to finish and see the kids happy. My career is the best thing. One more, to be able to teach the level that I want, my preference. I feel so lucky because I was able to work with those kids. I'm a kid-friendly person. I want to try different things with different kids. Kids are very smart, they absorb easily, they are imaginative, they are also experimenting. It's more interesting for me. You can manipulate them at that age!

Compared with the other teachers we have met in the previous chapters, Anna Marie does not appear to have experienced any prejudice at all. That is not to say that she has not struggled: moving to Japan as a young wife where she had to adapt to Japanese culture and take on the responsibilities of caring for two children in addition to her own. Like Lori and Sampaguita, Anna Marie was not a teacher before coming to Japan. There are other similarities with their stories: as with Lori, English teaching was not something she even considered before coming to Japan. Anna Marie learned about the possibility by chance through her connection with her colleague Alexia at the Outback restaurant, who turned out to be Aurora's daughter. Similarly, as with Sampaguita, she started working in business, although, unlike Sampaguita who chose to go into business for financial reasons, Anna Marie studied business administration and computer science at university in the Philippines because this was what her peers were doing; she had no clear idea of her own.

A striking feature of Anna Marie's story is how much she has invested in a teaching career, attending (and paying for) courses even when she was unable to work. The turning point in her life was her first encounter with FETJ and since then she has been 'actively' involved. The constraints on her seem to come mainly from her husband: he did not want her to work while she was pregnant and nursing a baby, and he is unhappy that she is now involved in so much teaching work. Anna Marie's way around this constraint is to prove to her husband that she can work and fulfil her domestic role as a wife (*'I'm showing him I that I can do my best as a mom and as a wife while keeping all these jobs'*).

Anna Marie's narrative is filled with emotionally charged language: English was her 'passion' when she was at school, and teaching is her passion now, and working with people who are not passionate is something she hates (*'it sucks'*). There is a hint of personal pride in the way she talks about her job at the international school and the social cachet of the people who send their children there (*'You know, International School is very expensive. Most of our students are sons and daughters of TV personalities'*). Interestingly, there is a hint of national pride too in her criticism of teachers she describes as 'not devoted, not passionate, not sincere in what they are doing'. Such teachers contrast with her own experience of kindergarten in the Philippines (*'all the teachers were very friendly'*). Another emotion that Anna Marie expresses at various points in her narrative is gratitude. She is 'grateful' to people who have helped her in her teaching career – to Aurora, the parents who sent their children to her for English lessons and to FETJ – because they all recognise her value or potential value as an English language teacher.

Next, I introduce Shin, the only man among the teachers in this book. I met Shin in 2015 at an FETJ party that he was organising at a

Filipino restaurant in one of Tokyo's southern wards. Loud music was interspersed with singing, dancing and comic skits by FETJ members and their children. I took the opportunity to sit with Shin in an upstairs storeroom and record his story of success.

Shin's Story

I'm half Filipino and half Japanese, my father is Japanese and my mother is Filipino. I went to elementary school, high school and college in the Philippines, but every holiday, every family event, wedding and so on, we came here, and every time there was some trouble, like there was a volcanic eruption, we all had to come here. We went back and forth. It was my parents' decision to have me educated in the Philippines. My father has three degrees and he's well aware of the education system in the Philippines, so he decided. I went to Far Eastern University and graduated in 2004 in Commerce.

I came here after college. In the Philippines at college I was very busy, very active on the student council, so I decided to have a vacation after graduation. But I then started looking for a job and that's how I started work in IT. I went back to the Philippines in 2007 because my sister had cancer and then I started working for Safeway, the US supermarket chain, in their IT department. They sent me to Arizona and California, so I loved that, I love Safeway, love their products. When my sister died, I came back here and Sharp rehired me. After working for them for two or three years, I started feeling stressed. You know how it is here, I was working in the office for 12 hours a day and I didn't have any social life. So I was thinking of changing and at that time I went to a teaching seminar. It was not long after that that I was hired to teach.

To tell the truth, it was my childhood dream to become a teacher. In the Philippines, if you're a teacher, you're not going to get a good salary. That's why I took commerce. If you work in sales or something you can earn money to make a living in the Philippines. But teaching was what I really wanted to do. So I found out that the teaching seminar was in my city. I don't live in Tokyo, I live in Mie. They had a seminar and I fell in love with it. I really like Miss Aurora. She gave me a push, she gave me inspiration. She told me, 'What are you doing? You should be teaching, you're a star!' So I did, I applied for a job with Interac and I told them that I wanted to work in Tokyo.

When I was at college in the Philippines, we did a lot of charity events with children. Even if the government says education is free, you still have to pay for clothes and things, so the student council that I was involved with put on charity events and we did teaching so poor children could read and write. So that was my only teaching experience. It's a little bit challenging because the education system here is different. Also the English is different 'cos in the Philippines everything is in English.

Here, it's English as a Second Language. But I told them I'm willing to be trained and I took some online courses. I took a course 'Shaping the Way to Teach English', it's like TESOL, but it's not TESOL, by the University of Oregon. So how to assess yourself as a teacher, how to manage a class, how to know the kids are learning. We had to make a lesson plan, and then do a demo lesson, so they are watching me in Oregon while I do the teaching demo: 'Hello from Tokyo!' It was a nice course.

Last year I was teaching in Meguro in elementary schools, and this year, here in Ota-ku. I'm working in two elementary schools and one junior high. I love elementary class, it's so much fun. What I do, sometimes there's no games, so I incorporate games. My technique with ESL is very student-focused. I don't do so much talking since they won't understand. I incorporate lots of games and songs. I'll say, 'How are you?' and they say 'I'm fine thank you', you know like a robot, but I'll say, 'No come on, everyone say something different: "I'm happy" or "I'm sad"'. So we start off with a game or a chat. Then I do the introduction of my lesson, for example, if it's sports, then we'll do another activity and then at the end another one, so three activities in the class.

In the junior high school, I'm just an assistant teacher. Usually I have a meeting first, and the teacher will ask me to prepare an activity, and I'll do that and sometimes just read something, that's her style. Usually they give me 20 minutes and I'll do a game. We don't sing, but if I play a One Direction song, we can do something as a warm-up. With Interac they give you a schedule before you go to the school. First period there will be the target language, the page on the book and there will be a note saying you can have 20 minutes. So it will be on the schedule and she will come to my table and we will talk about it. Or sometimes, they give me a paper, check this, this is a speech, check the grammar or spelling. With elementary, I have the whole 45 minutes, which I love, and I can do anything.

Last year when I was hired, I only went to one school, and the contract ends when the school year ends. But they renew the contract. It depends on the performance. Interac is the biggest dispatch company in Japan. I'm very satisfied with the company. We have meetings once a month. We discuss news, changes with the company, it's open for questions or problems. Problems? Usually it's with the Japanese teacher. One guy from England was complaining that the Japanese teacher was translating every word he said. So that's not good, right? The kids are not listening to you, they're only listening to the teacher translating. Also, one complaint is with the Special Needs class. In this class they combine everyone from grade 1 to 6, which is challenging for us because there is a big difference between the younger and older. The problem is that this is the Japanese system, it's just this year they are starting English lessons on this scale, so they still have problems to solve. That's why it's good that we have communication with the company, because they don't know what is happening in the schools.

Interac is amazing. Before they send you out, they will give you a training. We do a lot of drills at the office. Two weeks of training for the lesson plans and the books and everything. The company has given me a lot of support. If there is anything I don't know, I send an email and they send an answer right away. For instance, grammar: they'll give me a way to explain it. And they have a database, and everything is there. All the flash cards, activities. You just have to print them out. Basically, I'm getting all my teaching techniques from my company.

FETJ changed my life. I was a regular salaryman leading a boring life. The teaching seminar helped me to change that. As a sign of gratitude, I've been secretary of Kanagawa Chapter since last year, and this year I just hosted this event, it was my idea. I'm giving everything to them, they helped me, so I'm paying forward. If you say 'Filipino', if you go to other countries, people will think 'domestic helpers', right? So this is a way to use our English proficiency. I want to help other Filipinos and lift the image of Filipinos.

My own identity? I'm always half. When I was living in the Philippines, I'm not Filipino, 'Shinichi, that's the Japanese guy'. And here, I'm not Japanese, I'm the Filipino guy. And also living as a gay. Oh my god, it's a struggle. But I'm a positive person, I don't think about what's negative, what's bad. So if my parents want me to live in the Philippines, let's go. But I wanted to pay back my parents for my education. I always graduate with honours. I want to make them proud. And now that I'm living my dream, they're proud of that too.

What I love about teaching, when you're the teacher, you don't have to be the manager. Actually, Interac is offering me to be a head teacher. But this means evaluating other teachers and that means I don't get to teach any more. I want to teach in schools, that's what I want. Maybe in 10 years I'll be a teacher, and then maybe I'll have a school of my own. Right now, I'm 30 years old. I want to work, but after my work I want to be with my friends. I don't need that responsibility, or that money right now. Right now, I'm very happy to teach in the morning, then to go out to a movie in the evening, and to go out in the weekend.

The hardest thing is dealing with Japanese teachers. For me it's OK. There's this one teacher, she's micromanaging everything. The company is well aware, they're asking, 'Is she stressing you out?' But I can't change her, that's the way it is, she's different, I'm different, I have to respect that. 'The other classes are lucky because you are not there. They are having fun'. But I don't care about her. The kids are awesome. She's very traditional.

If the kids start talking to me in English, that's the best thing. My advantage is that I look Japanese and my name is Japanese. They always talk to me, most of the time in Japanese, but I go, 'What?' and then they try. I'm very happy if they say even one word. It's going to be memorable for them. I'm very happy if they give you some simple notes in English. I frame everything, even if it's just a small origami.

Although Shin is the only man in this study, I wanted to include him for the perspectives and insights his story provides for thinking about national identity and gender identity in English language teacher identity. Not '*nissei*' or '*sansei*' (as Sampaguita defines herself because of her Japanese grandfather), Shin describes himself as '*always half*'. This hybrid identity, referred to as '*hafu*' in Japan (Kamada, 2009), renders him vulnerable to 'othering', whether he is in the Philippines or in Japan ('*"Shinichi, that's the Japanese guy". And here, I'm not Japanese, I'm the Filipino guy*'). But, in contrast with much of the literature that attests to the disadvantages of being Japanese or Asian (e.g. Houghton & Rivers, 2013; Kubota & Fujimoto, 2013), Shin finds it works to his advantage as an English teacher. With a Japanese name and as a Japanese language speaker, he feels the children can relate to him more easily. In her study of mixed-ethnic adolescent girls in Japan, Kamada (2009) coins the term *ethno-gendering* to describe how the girls accomplish and manage their identities, and how this can come into conflict with how they are seen by others. In a similar vein, Shin hints at how both his mixed-ethnic identity and sexual identity as 'gay' have to be managed in what could be perilous waters ('*Oh my god, it's a struggle*'). But he also stresses that he is a 'positive person' ('*I don't think about what's negative, what's bad*'), and so construes what could be regarded as disadvantages as advantages.

There are a number of similarities between Shin's story and the narratives of the Filipino women. Like them, Shin accepts without question the constraints put on him by his family. In his younger life, he moved back and forth between Japan and the Philippines, driven to Japan by volcanoes in the Philippines, or his Japanese father's decision to educate him in the Philippines, or the illness and death of his sister ('*if my parents want me to live in the Philippines, let's go*'). Like the women, too, Shin invests in his teaching career: by undertaking an online course with the University of Oregon, and by his involvement with FETJ. As in Elma's story, pride for Shin is a family matter. He wants to 'pay (his parents) back' for giving him a college education and he does so by excelling in what he does ('*I always graduate with honours. I want to make them proud. And now that I'm living my dream, they're proud of that too*'). Apart from the 'othering' that he experiences in both Japan and the Philippines because of his mixed family, Shin also makes a very interesting observation about attitudes towards Filipinos and the role he can play in the enhancement of their reputation ('*If you say "Filipino", if you go to other countries, people will think "domestic helpers", right? So this is a way to use our English proficiency. I want to help other Filipinos and lift the image of Filipinos*').

As we saw in previous chapters, Filipinos are not admitted into Japan to work as domestic helpers, as they are to places such as the oil-rich countries of the Middle East or to Singapore. The image of Filipinos in Japan is arguably worse than this, or at least, it has been in the relatively recent past. But Shin draws on a type of discourse originating in the Philippines that vaunts the state policy of producing 'workers of the world', assuming Filipino overseas workers to be worth more than other migrants because of their supposed proficiency in English (Lorente, 2012, 2017). Shin does not see himself as this type of Filipino, but he is sensitive to the global stereotype of Filipinos and buys into the assumption that the negative image can be changed through work associated with English.

Shin's career trajectory, however, contrasts strikingly with that of the women. Graduating with a degree in commerce from a prestigious university in the Philippines, Shin works first for a Japanese multinational electronics company, and then for an American retail company in the Philippines, before returning to the Sharp Corporation after his sister's death and his return to Japan. In terms of money and status, Shin was on the path to a highly prestigious career. His decision to change to English teaching in Japan could be seen as a big step down. But Shin justifies the move by the fact that the Sharp job was consuming too much of his time, denying him the chance to enjoy a social life. He justifies it, too, by asserting that teaching had been his childhood dream, and that his parents are proud of him for fulfilling this dream. Moreover, Shin's new career as a teacher of English appears to be providing him with opportunities for rapid progression, if he wants it, which he claims he does not. Shin has only positive things to say about his employer, the dispatch company Interac, praising it for the training and support it gives him and for its willingness to listen to employees' views about problems and difficulties working in schools (for a contrasting view, see Currie-Robson [2015]). The company, in turn, appears to view Shin very positively too, offering him a promotion to 'head teacher', overseeing and training other teachers. Shin turns down this managerial role, since he wants to enjoy teaching for the time being, yet he sees that he is likely to move to this kind of position in the future. Like Anna Marie, Shin's dynamic personality and enthusiasm for teaching shine through his story. Two stories are not enough to generalise about gender in English language teaching (ELT) in Japan; but where Anna Marie accepts all opportunities of work in addition to fulfilling all her duties as a wife and mother, Shin is relaxed enough to refuse such offers, confident that he will have more opportunities for advancement in the future. Can this difference be explained by gender?

Like Anna Marie, Shin attributes his success in becoming an English teacher to FETJ ('*FETJ changed everything*') and he is grateful for the special recognition that Aurora accorded him ('*She gave me a push, she gave me inspiration. She told me, "What are you doing? You should be teaching, you're a star!'"*). As with Anna Marie, it is gratitude that motivates Shin to continue to be involved with FETJ, as secretary of one of the larger chapters, and as organiser of the party where I met him and recorded his story. Money metaphors occur twice in Shin's story: first when he says he wanted to pay his parents back for their support of him through his education, and secondly when he explains his involvement with FETJ (*'I'm giving everything to them, they helped me, so I'm paying forward'*). Shin's commitment to FETJ is expressed as a kind of currency: he receives help, so feels an obligation to 'pay forward', and help others who come after him. But teaching itself is a kind of occupation in which the currency of altruism may be as much of a reward as monetary income – at least, it may in Japan where the salary of a teacher is enough to live on.

I turn now to the third of the young teachers, Katrina, whose story provides yet another perspective. Katrina was also at the party in Kanagawa where I interviewed Shin, and she agreed to tell me her story sitting in the storeroom above the restaurant.

Katrina's Story

I came to Japan in January 2011, just before the earthquake. I was in Saitama applying for jobs at the time of the earthquake. I got a call from Minerva Language Institute saying I was hired just two days before the earthquake and I was really worried if I would still have the job after the quake. I was thinking of going home but my parents wanted to stay in Japan, and it would be unfair if I go alone.

My mum came to Japan in the year 2000 and married a Japanese, so my stepdad is Japanese. He adopted me. First time I came to Japan I was 17, and then I had to get a permanent visa so I had to stay for two years. I stopped studying and stayed here for that. So I went to work with my mum in a food factory, slicing meat, bacon for food chains. That was my first experience of work in Japan. So when I got my long-term visa I went back to the Philippines to finish my education, then came back again to apply for a permanent resident visa, and I got that as soon as I applied.

I finished college, so I have a bachelor's degree in family economics, majoring in food management with a minor in education. That meant taking 18 credits in education and that would enable me to get a teaching license. There were only a few who took the education license exam, as most people wanted to continue in the food industry. But I thought that doing the 18 credits in education was a win-win situation. If I pass it, I'm lucky, if not, so be it, at least I tried. But fortunately I passed so I have a license to be a high school teacher. But I didn't get any teaching experience in the Philippines as I came to Japan straight after graduation.

I applied to Minerva online, but before that I already knew about FETJ. When I first came, I didn't know where to start. I applied by myself online to millions of companies but got no reply. Then one day, I thought of calling one of my mum's friends, Anna Marie, and she said, 'Come to a grammar workshop tomorrow'. I hadn't registered or anything, but I went along. I'd already met Aurora's daughter through Anna Marie so then I met Aurora and she was like a knight in shining armour. I realized, wow, I can have a career in Japan. So I joined FETJ and went to workshops. And then I got the offer from Minerva.

So I started teaching young learners, from two to 12 or 13 years old. I had very few classes, just after school classes. Minerva have their own lesson plans that we have to follow. Depending on the students' needs, we can do different things provided we cover the target language. During that time, we had personal training by Aurora. Even before I was hired, she prepared me for the interviews, she explained how to do lesson demos, she taught us different activities, how to do resumes. I'm really grateful for what she has done for me. I was lucky, because there were only a few members then.

After Minerva, I wanted to challenge myself, so I applied to the Fujimi Board of Education. I wanted to try teaching junior high school working Monday to Friday so that I could join the FETJ workshops at the weekend. They were looking for only one teacher. At the time, I thought that they would really prefer a native speaker, and they wanted two years of experience. But I thought there's no harm in trying, and submitted my resume and got a call, and did a demo. They asked me what BoE I applied for and they rang me to say they would let me know in two weeks and if I was applying for other BoEs. Of course I was, I said, I needed to get a job. So then they rang again and asked if I had to choose, would I choose Fujimi City, and I said, 'Yes of course'. So then they gave me the job straight away.

Teaching junior high school was very different to Minerva. In Minerva you were the main teacher. In junior high school, there were some teachers, especially old teachers, who just use you as a recorder. But younger teachers used me as a main teacher. But I got a little bored, so I started applying for elementary schools because I wanted to make my own teaching plans. So I started teaching in Toda City, fortunately elementary students. In Toda City, it's one school one ALT. Every week we have lessons, unlike Minerva. I could really see the improvement of my students, which was much more fulfilling.

In Toda they encourage expansion of speaking activities. In Minerva we would teach, 'How's the weather?' But in Toda, we'd teach 'How's the weather in different places around the world?' Toda City wanted us to introduce the students to different cultures. The ALTs in Toda are not from one country, but from many different countries. So students become familiar with different accents. We do team teaching and every morning we meet the teachers and discuss what we're going to do. I encourage the homeroom teacher to help with pronouncing the words. And then *we have training every Monday. We share ideas, so every teacher has to share their idea. The students are really enthusiastic. So by sixth grade they can answer any question. In Toda we have interview test for the students, from third grade to sixth grade. They get the data from us and they submit it to the Board of Education. They show the results of the interview test and we discuss how we can improve it.*

I'm really grateful that I got this job, where we are listened to. We are able to talk about the situation at the school, any problems, and everyone gives input. It's really helpful. Most of the teachers have problems with team teaching. Some Japanese teachers do not really cooperate. They are there to discipline the students. Most of us want them to be a model for the students, like do demos. But there are teachers who put it all on us. Another is Japanese teachers underestimate the students. 'This is too difficult, the students can't do this'. They are afraid that we will introduce things that are too difficult. But we want to add things that are not in the books.

With FETJ at first I was an active member, and then they appointed me as an officer, so now I'm responsible for the membership of the organization. So they have given me major roles. But the most interesting role is being a teacher trainer. It helps develop my social skills. My life has drastically changed since doing that. I've met many people, not only teachers, but professors, it's nice to know more people who are more experienced. If there are things I don't know, I just have to ask. I have learned a lot just from asking.

The hardest thing is when students are not interested in learning. There are students who think, I'm not going to trouble myself, I don't need this. I was shocked, because in the Philippines kids never disrespect teachers. If kids are angry, they are angry with their actions but never with speaking out, unlike here. They'll say, 'Urusai!' ['Shut up'], I never heard anything like that in the Philippines. Or you try to help them and they go, 'Iranai!' ['I don't want your help']. For me, because of my cultural background, it's not acceptable. The Japanese teachers don't react to that. But I get really angry inside. That was the first problem I brought to the BoE, and they said we have no right to discipline the students. They said, 'You'll get used to it'. So I ignored it. But at elementary school, they are all really nice, though sometimes a bit overexcited and running round the classroom.

The most gratifying thing is when students can answer my questions right away in the review at the beginning of the class, it makes me feel like I'm effective. And then at the end, I ask them to perform something and everyone volunteers, and I love that. They're confident enough to try and to speak the way I do. That's very fulfilling.

As an ALT, I can't really see a clear vision of where my career is going. I want to be an educator. I plan to study more, take a master's degree, maybe try to be a lecturer in a university in the Philippines or maybe in Japan. I'm going to be the coordinator of Jolly English – I can't teach in Toda City, because the BoE won't let me teach in other places – they're very possessive. So Aurora asked me to coordinate the teachers. We're going to start with just two teachers for trial classes. Sometimes in FETJ, there are difficult times, it's time-consuming. But I see Aurora doing all these things, so I think, well, if she can do it, then I should try. Time management is hard, but we have to prioritise things. Membership is hard because I ask for members' names from the chapters, and they delay, and so when Aurora asks me, I can't deliver, and then I feel that I'm not good at this. But she says that it's OK, that everyone is a volunteer and we can't force people.

Katrina is the youngest of the teachers, but she has been working a couple of years longer than Anna Marie and Shin. Unlike them, she had experience of working in a factory, leaving high school in the Philippines to work with her mother slicing bacon in a food processing plant in Japan. Katrina's story makes explicit the priority of securing legal residence in Japan above her education. Only when she had a long-term visa, did she return to the Philippines to finish high school and college. She includes in her story the detail that she applied for and got permanent residence in Japan when she returned, as the adopted daughter of a Japanese citizen. Ensuring the right to reside in Japan still comes before a career.

Another point of contrast in Katrina's story is that she initially applied for teaching jobs by herself, thinking that her teaching qualification from the Philippines would be sufficient. Only when her numerous applications were ignored did she approach FETJ, through Anna Marie and Aurora's daughter Alexia. Anna Marie and Shin claimed that FETJ was the factor that launched their careers as English teachers in Japan; in Katrina's case, we can see that this was indeed the case. Access to English teaching jobs for Filipinos may have eased since the mid-1980s when Elma first arrived in Japan, but at the time Katrina returned to Japan looking for teaching work, it was still relatively restricted. In addition to a high school teaching license, Katrina needed the added value of a certificate of training from FETJ and an endorsement from Aurora. Katrina takes it for granted that her Filipino identity weighs against her, so when she applies for a job with a board of education, she is surprised that not only is she accepted, but also two different boards of education vie with each other to recruit her, despite the fact that she is not a 'native speaker' and lacks experience as a teacher.

A further point of contrast is that Katrina has had more varied experience as a teacher, having worked as an assistant language teacher (ALT) for three different organisations: for the dispatch company Minerva, which sent her to various elementary schools allowing for limited continuity and thus little chance to get to know her students; for the Fujimi Board of Education, which sent her to junior high schools; and finally for the Toda City Board of Education, where she works in her most fulfilling job so far as an elementary school ALT. This variety has enabled her to evaluate those jobs: Minerva allowed her to teach elementary classes by herself, whereas the Fujimi Board of Education stipulated that she follow a strict plan. Toda City Board of Education was better than Minerva because the board encouraged expansion of speaking activities and wanted teachers to include cultural content. Katrina also has experience of teaching older students who are not interested in English and are disrespectful to her, behaviour that she compares unfavourably with that of students in the Philippines, and with that of elementary school students who are enthusiastic about English.

Like Shin, Katrina has worked with Japanese teachers who do not want to, or do not know how to, make use of an ALT. In the narratives of Lori and Shin, who also work in public schools, as well as in the findings of previous studies on ALTs and team teaching in Japan (Carless, 2006; McConnell, 2000; Tajino & Tajino, 2000; Turnbull, 2018), some dissatisfaction is expressed, either directly or implicitly, with the role imposed on them by the homeroom teacher. All the Filipino teachers here are happiest when they are free to teach 'solo', and most dissatisfied when their role is reduced to merely reading aloud from the textbook. These two extremes may be typical of what Shin refers to as 'traditional' Japanese teachers who resist ceding any control to the ALTs. Control, in the sense of discipline, is an issue that Katrina raises with the board of education, only to be told that she has no such authority in the classroom. Nevertheless, there is an interesting reversal in the attitude that Katrina (and her ALT colleagues) take towards the Japanese homeroom teachers: ('*Most of us want them to be a model for the students, like do demos*'). In the traditional classroom, power is the preserve of the homeroom teacher and the Japanese language. Katrina's desire that the homeroom teachers act as models of English may reflect a changing attitude within official English teaching policy, but this is contradicted by the reality in the classroom of traditional teachers, a grammar-based curriculum and an emphasis on testing and university entrance exams (Gordon *et al.*, 2010). As Turnbull (2018) points out, the job of an ALT is to be an assistant in the classroom, an institutional identity that contradicts the pedagogical role of the teachers in communicative classrooms. At least, like Shin, Katrina is able to voice these frustrations at meetings organised by her board of education, and she is grateful that her views are listened to.

Katrina has more to say about her role in FETJ. More than just providing her with access to teaching jobs, her involvement in FETJ has introduced her to a wide range of people and widened her horizon of possible career development. Like Anna Marie, she is about to embark on a new venture, as a coordinator of one of the two Jolly English schools that FETJ is about to open, a commercial *eikaiwa* in which FETJ members would be able to get actual teaching practice in 'trial classes'. Unlike Anna Marie and Shin, Katrina admits to some doubts about her own abilities. As an officer in charge of membership for FETJ, she finds it difficult to get information from the local chapters and feels disappointed in herself for being unable to fulfil that role as she should, or as she would like to. Aurora consoles her with the fact that everyone in FETJ is a volunteer and 'you cannot force people'. In Chapter 4, we saw Sampaguita's viewpoint on the need to create and maintain structure in FETJ. Aurora's comment, as reported by Katrina, highlights the difficulty in striking a balance between keeping order and keeping members willing. This is obviously no easy task. Katrina is motivated to continue because of her admiration of and loyalty to Aurora ('*I see Aurora doing all these things, so I think, well if she can do it, then I should try*'). As with Anna Marie and Shin, such emotions play a fundamental role in Katrina's commitment to the group and to her sense of what it means to be a good teacher.

Having introduced three teachers who are still at the start of their teaching careers and having commented on the emotions that they express in their narratives, I turn now to some more theoretical questions regarding work and identity.

Is ELT a Career?

In my own story, I recounted how I started teaching English as a 'career' at a relatively late stage in my life after moving to Japan, although I had taught English as a part-time job at English language schools during my undergraduate and graduate studies in the United Kingdom. I was fortunate to begin my career in Japan as a university teacher, a relatively high-status position to which many English teachers aspire (including, as we saw in her narrative, Katrina). Perhaps it is because the last 25 years of my life have followed an upward trajectory in terms of status and salary that I can feel some justification in calling it a career. Within the teaching English to speakers of other languages (TESOL) field, however, there is far less certainty about whether ELT is a career or not. Johnston (1997), who posed the question – perhaps somewhat provocatively – in the first place, was sceptical and showed that the Polish teachers of English in his study did not talk about their work in such terms. Teachers are complex individuals, Johnston (1997: 708) argued, and they inhabit complex contexts 'in which personal, educational political and socioeconomic discourses all influence the way the life is told'.

The Polish teachers in Johnston's study may not have thought of their English teaching work as careers, but other researchers have shown that many language teachers do think of their working lives in this way. Hayes' (2005) life stories of three Sri Lankan teachers follow a distinct career progression through to retirement, while Cheung (2005) showed that secondary school English language teachers in Hong Kong envisaged a similar progression, albeit with many variations. The notion of a career may thus be most meaningful in the institutional context of formal education. In many countries, including Japan, public school teachers are civil servants and, as such, are highly regarded socially (although with increasing challenges to their status and authority) and assured tenure throughout their working lives. As we have seen, foreign ALTs in Japan do not have this status, although private schools can – and many do – hire foreigners under the same conditions as Japanese. Furthermore, as many of the Filipino teachers' stories reveal, the institutions that hire teachers can impose widely varying terms of employment, ranging from the precarious short-term contracts of some dispatch companies, which themselves are subject to short-term contracts with local boards of education, to full-time employment with schools with higher remuneration, more autonomy in the classroom and more responsibility within the school community. Anna Marie has fallen on her feet in this regard, securing a job in a prestigious international pre-school straight from running her own private classes (compare this with Lori's experience). Significantly, she says '*I'm not an English teacher, I'm a schoolteacher*', a role that puts her at the centre of the school community, compared with the marginal place usually assigned to language teachers (Linville & Whiting, 2019).

Apart from the institutional identity of schoolteacher, does language teacher constitute a professional identity in which the notion of a career trajectory makes sense? Garton and Richards (2008: xiv) argue that it does, that TESOL can be thought of 'as a profession [that is] temporally as well as geographically compartmentalised'. Adapting Huberman's (1993) four stages of a teacher career trajectory: (1) starting out (survival/discovery); (2) becoming experienced (stabilisation); (3) new horizons (experimentation/reassessment); and (4) passing on the knowledge (serenity/relational distance), Garton and Richards organise the chapters in their anthology to explore the discourses that English language teachers encounter at various stages in their working lives. If we try to map this framework onto the careers of the Filipino teachers, however, we notice some contradictions that give rise to some awkward questions.

Aurora and Elma, for example, were teachers in the Philippines (of speech communication and of business management) before they became English teachers, and their induction into English teaching in Japan seems to have been conducted by the companies they worked for rather than via any separate training or education. Viewed in terms of Garton and Richards' framework, should we consider their careers in Japan as separate from their previous teaching careers, or as a continuation, albeit at a lower level?

Sampaguita reveals how important it is for FETJ to keep control of the practices that are passed on in training new members and the role of trainer is limited to a small number of people, including some of the younger teachers, such as Anna Marie and Katrina. Accordingly, to be critical of FETJ's emphasis on control, where does the third stage of experimentation feature in this scheme? And to be critical of Garton and Richards' (2008) four-stage model, why does passing on knowledge only feature at the end of a career trajectory? What, indeed, is meant by 'passing on knowledge'? Would it not include the meetings that Shin attends with his employer Interac, and Katrina attends with the board of education, in which their knowledge of the actual classroom conditions and suggestions for improved practice are respected and valued?

The notion of a career as an upward trajectory that passes through different stages as practitioners accumulate knowledge and expertise (Tsui, 2003) may be outdated and, as I have already indicated, limited in its application, for example to large, traditional institutions or to public sector education in which teachers are regarded as civil servants. However, even these areas of work are increasingly affected by the 'new work order' (Gee et al., 1996) in which we all live. Gee et al. (1996) define this new work order as the 'discourse of managers', a discourse that promises 'work that is more satisfying and meaningful, greater respect for diversity, and more democratic distribution of knowledge'. Sociologists Luc Boltanski and Eve Chiapello (2017) have termed this 'the new spirit of capitalism' to describe the discourse and the nature of work that has emerged since the late 1960s, a spirit that 'valorizes projects, creativity, network existence, the need to become a self-entrepreneur, and new corporate figures like the coach or project head'. Similarly, as I discussed earlier, Block (2018) has argued that the neoliberal subject sees herself as an entrepreneur, responsible for the project of enhancing her own human capital through a 'portfolio career' (Handy, 2015) and of marketing this capital through self-branding. This is a system where the ties of commitment by employers to employees and vice versa are loosened by the priorities of rational economic choice. We can see this reflected in the shift in the recruitment of ALTs from boards of education to dispatch companies, creating a new stratum of English language teachers, employed on lower salaries and on more precarious terms. We can also see it reflected in the behaviour of Anna Marie, Shin and Katrina, three successful teachers who are negotiating their way up through the system, putting up with bad conditions in order to leverage their way up to the next, better job.

Financial concerns are indeed evident in many of the teachers' stories. For example, Shin claims that he always wanted to become a teacher but explains that he did not choose this path because 'in the Philippines, if you're a teacher, you're not going to get a good salary'. Similarly, Sampaguita relates that teaching had been her dream also but her family was poor, 'that's why I went to secretarial school: I could get a good salary quite quickly'. Nevertheless, a financial motive does not adequately explain the strong emotions that they express about teaching, and in the case of Anna Marie, about English. How then are we to explain these FETJ teachers' commitment not only to their paid work, but to their unpaid work for FETJ? One way to answer this is to view work in more than merely economic terms.

Market, Social and Moral Spheres of Work

The sociologist Keith Grint (2005: 2) makes the point that work belongs to a social and moral sphere as well as to a market sphere. I would argue that in teaching generally, the social and moral rewards are more attractive than the prospect of financial gain. This is brought into sharp relief in Shin's decision to change career from a well-paid, high-status job with a large multinational company for which he was obliged to work 12-hour days to a job as an ALT, for considerably less pay and with lower social status, but which gives him more time for a social life and the freedom to move from provincial Mie to the capital city Tokyo. We saw this also in Lori's story, in her passing observation that she was earning a lot of money working in bars and did not expect that teaching would be as lucrative.

The social sphere refers to the social context of work as English teachers. In Anna Marie's case, the international school where she works as a kindergarten teacher appears to be a source of satisfaction and pride. Not only is the school a 'fun' place to work, but it also has high social cachet. As Anna Marie mentions, one of her students is the son of a famous singer, while another student is the child of a famous baseball player. In the case of Shin and Katrina, the schools themselves may not be wholly satisfactory. Both of them describe problems: with a Japanese homeroom teacher (Shin), or with disaffected teenagers (Katrina), but both speak in glowing terms of the elementary school students they teach. Additionally, both of them speak positively about their employers, Interac in Shin's case, and the Toda Board of Education in Katrina's, for the opportunities that they provide not only for professional development, but also for them to voice their own experiences and opinions.

However, over and above the places where they work, the most important social sphere for these three teachers is FETJ. The mission statement on FETJ's website not only states that its purpose is to train teachers and help them to find jobs in Japan, but it also claims to be a 'catalyst' in enhancing the quality of life for Filipinos living in Japan, which it does through a busy calendar of social events, such as parties, festivals, celebrations, picnics and so on. Socially, FETJ is a community in which these young teachers could feel an immediate sense of belonging because of their national and cultural identity. A similar sense of belonging is expressed by Anna Marie when she relates how finding a Filipino community at church 'changed everything' for her after a long period of struggle and isolation as a new wife in Japan. However, it is not merely the cultural connection that attracts these teachers; each of them is highly active in FETJ. They go out of their way to contribute to the success of the group. A major factor for this strong connection in all three cases is the role that is played by Aurora. Each of them expresses gratitude to Aurora and explains their continued involvement in FETJ as a debt of loyalty to her. Shin, interestingly, explains his motivation to succeed in all his endeavours as paying a debt, Thus, in the case of his parents, he wishes to pay them back for their support of him growing up. In the case of FETJ, he declares that he is 'paying it forward': for the support he received in changing his career from office work to English teaching, he devotes his free time to supporting other Filipino would-be English teachers. Thus, FETJ is not merely an important social sphere for these teachers, but it is also a moral sphere in which they are motivated by emotions of gratitude, obligation and doing what is right.

The moral sphere is, of course, especially salient when the narrators talk about teaching practice. These are the moments in the narratives when the strongest emotions are expressed. As we saw in Chapter 3, Lori is upset about the American teacher at the teacher training course not just because she was frightened into silence by the woman's anger, but also because she believed that the teacher's attitude, her inability to laugh at herself, was inappropriate for someone who works with children. In Chapter 4, Sampaguita is upset about the children who sleep during English class because she believes they have been ignored and neglected by their teachers, and she makes the effort to pay special attention to them. In this chapter, moral indignation also appears, as in the case of Sampaguita, as a clash of cultural values. Anna Marie is upset about teachers who are not genuine or kind to children and avers that such attitudes would be unthinkable in kindergarten teachers in the Philippines. Katrina for her part is upset that disaffected teenagers in her class are disrespectful to her and that she has no right to chastise them for their rudeness. What is common to each of these examples is the passionate conviction each teacher holds about what they feel is right or wrong when it comes to teaching children. Of the economic, social and moral spheres of teaching English in Japan, it is the moral sphere that evokes the strongest emotion among the narrators and that best explains their 'passion' to be English teachers.

Morality, Advocacy and Recognition

Brian Morgan and Matthew Clark (2011: 825) have written that 'perhaps the most significant development in language teacher identity research is the turn towards values, morals and ethics'. An important landmark in this turn towards morality in language teaching is Bill Johnston's (2003) *Values in English Language Teaching*. According to Johnston (2003: 1), 'language teaching is a profoundly value-laden activity', since unlike any other subject, it is 'international virtually by definition and thus cannot comfortably rest its morality on conventional national cultural models (even setting aside the problematic nature of such models)' (Johnston, 2003: 20). Throughout this book, I have tended to use the word 'value', as have many other researchers (see Chapter 3), in its economic sense as a synonym of 'worth'. Johnston (2003: 10), however, takes values 'to refer to beliefs about what is right and good', a definition that he also assigns to morality. The theoretical basis of Johnston's thinking comes from the work of the educational philosopher Nel Noddings (1984) who sees morality as inherent not in individuals but in the relation between them. According to Noddings (1984: 4), a basic fact of human existence is 'human encounter and affective response' and a primary moral impulse is the unequal relationship of caring.

We can see positive expressions of caring in the narratives in Sampaguita's efforts to pay special attention to the students who sleep through the English class and in Shin's collection and framing of the little gifts he receives from his students. We see caring too in Aurora's original initiative to help fellow Filipinos by starting the study group that grew into FETJ. More strikingly, however, morality is foregrounded when there is a conflict of values in the classroom, such as in Sampaguita's observation that the Japanese teachers let sleeping students be, or in Shin's frustration with the 'traditional', micromanaging teacher who does not let him do his job. But in the stories of the Filipino teachers, the attitude of caring is not only directed towards students, but it is also evident in expressions of loyalty towards Aurora, in particular, for her role in helping them to launch their teaching careers. The caring is mutual. This characteristic of the reciprocal caring relationships among members of the FETJ group is not unique to Filipinos; I see it in my own relationships with my students and my university colleagues in Japan, just as I do in other groups in which I play an active role. In terms of Honneth's (1995, 2012) social theory, recognition is manifested in the family sphere as love – caring by another name. Sampaguita refers to FETJ as it was when she first joined as 'a mother–daughter relationship' between Aurora and the younger members of the group. At all the events that I attended, Aurora constantly declared to the participants, 'I love you, my dear teachers', signalling her recognition of them as surrogate daughters, as well as recognising them as teachers, the identity that they desire and imagine.

Caring for others, however, is not the only way that morality has been defined by applied linguists. Phan Le Ha (2008), for example, places morality at the heart of teacher identity and identity formation. Her study of Vietnamese teachers who had completed master's degrees in Australia highlights dilemmas that arose for these teachers on their return to teaching practice in their home country. In Vietnamese society, where teachers are highly respected and regarded as 'moral guides', these Western-educated teachers needed to negotiate their identities anew. 'Unfastened' from their traditional education practices as a result of their experiences in Australia, they needed to 'refasten' themselves to identities as 'morality demonstrators' that were appropriate in the Vietnamese context. As Phan (2008: 185) states, 'in the context of mobility, transnationality, and the dominance of the Western academy, the role of teachers as moral guides becomes the most powerful element in the processes of identity formation'.

Phan's conclusions regarding the pivotal role of morality in teaching, and how language teachers are moral guides for their students, provide an interesting basis for comparison with the Filipino teachers. As I have sought to show, the emotional peaks in many of the narratives in this book concern moral dilemmas or moral judgements about teaching, and these are frequently associated with conflicts between what the narrators believe to be Filipino values and the values of Japanese or 'native-speaker' teachers. A major difference between Phan's narrators and the Filipino teachers is, of course, that the Vietnamese teachers return to work in Vietnam, whereas the Filipinos live and work in Japan. All the Filipino narrators in this book were educated in the Philippines, a country in which, like Vietnam, teachers are highly respected (as Katrina points out). Their beliefs about teaching and teachers were formed through an 'apprenticeship of observation' (Lortie, 1975) in the education system of the Philippines. However, unlike the Vietnamese teachers in Phan's study, although Anna Marie and Shin claim that they always wanted to be teachers, only Katrina actually trained and received a teaching certificate in the Philippines, and this only after her mother had moved to Japan and her residence there was assured. Although all three received an initial impetus to their teaching identity from FETJ, Anna Marie and Shin both went on to undertake TESOL courses to gain further valuable qualifications. Phan goes to some lengths to argue against essentialising identities, and yet, practically speaking, all her participants share experiences that lend themselves to essentialised binaries such as Western/ Vietnamese. The experience of these Filipino teachers and the identities that are implied are more complex: educated in the Philippines, trained in the 'Western academy' and teaching in Japan. Moreover, how does FETJ fit into these categories?

As I argued in Chapter 4, FETJ's formation as a language teacher association (LTA) has involved a struggle between two possible identities: one, a loose structure dominated by its charismatic leader Aurora, and the other, a more defined organisation governed by clearly defined executive roles and procedural regulations. I concluded that the latter identity had become more prominent, but it could also be argued that the identities of Aurora and the other teacher trainers remain of paramount importance to the group. In other words, it is precisely their complex hybrid identity as *Filipinos who are experienced as teachers of English in Japan* that attracts new members to the group. Individually, this identity enables them to act as role models for aspiring teachers. As a group, moreover, it enables FETJ to act as an advocate, awarding certificates to participants who complete its seminars and workshops, and recommending the most promising of them for jobs with local boards of education.

The role of advocacy in language education has recently come to prominence in English as a second language (ESL) contexts, where English language teachers are expected to advocate for learners and for fellow TESOL professionals (Linville & Whiting, 2019) (although see Morgan [2016] for a critical discussion of the effectiveness of such a move). The meaning of advocacy has been problematised by Harrison and Prado (2019), who distinguish between transformative advocacy that seeks to change the underlying conditions that led to a social injustice, and non-transformative advocacy that seeks merely to remediate the effects of the injustice without affecting the underlying conditions. As we saw in Chapter 4, under the leadership of Cesar Santoyo, Community and Home-based English Teachers (CHOBET)-FETJ had a more socially activist role in turning Filipino former entertainers into English teachers. However, although the ultimate objective was to improve the status of Filipinos in Japan, the means of advocacy was, I would argue, non-transformative. In its actions, the group took and continues to take advantage of existing, albeit evolving conditions, most notably, the increase in demand for teachers of English to younger children, the legal reform affecting the hiring of teachers and personal contacts in local boards of education. Nevertheless, through the training seminars and workshops, FETJ aims to develop excellent teachers whose subsequent work in the Japanese private and public education sectors will contribute to the widespread recognition of Filipinos as legitimate, competent and reliable teachers of English.

In this chapter, I have brought the story of FETJ to the present day with the narratives of three of the younger 'stars' in the group. Their stories provide the backdrop for a discussion of language teaching as work. In terms of a career, these three teachers are rising upwards from precarious, short-term jobs to more stable positions. They can be seen to exercise agency over the amount of work they undertake, for example, Anna Marie's declaration that she will show her husband she can do three jobs and still be a good wife and mother, and over the pace of their advancement, such as Shin's resistance to his company's offer of a head teacher role. Furthermore, following Grint (2005), I have looked at work as comprising not only economic, but also social and moral spheres. It is these latter aspects that are most vividly depicted in the narratives, and it is these aspects that explain not only these Filipino teachers' passion for teaching but also their loyalty and commitment to Aurora and to FETJ.

6 Different Perspectives

The final two stories are told by Filipino teachers of English in Japan who are not members of Filipino English Teacher in Japan (FETJ), although both have come into contact with the organisation in the past. Renata and Carmela now teach at the university level and Carmela also teaches Japanese students who will become teachers of English to young learners. Their stories, very different in their own way, provide a new perspective from which to explore the prejudice/pride trope, as well as a final collection of narrative data from which to reassess aspects of teacher identity that have been discussed in the previous chapters, namely national, ethnic and migrant identity, class identity and professional identity. Because Renata and Carmela are not members of FETJ, I examine the membership categories (Gray & Morton, 2018; Hogg & Reid, 2006) that they do invoke at various points as they position themselves in their narratives.

I met Renata in 2014 when I attended a talk she was giving about her research on Filipino migrants in Japan. Because her research was so closely linked to mine, I kept in touch with her afterwards and two years later collaborated with her on a forum at the Japan Association for Language Teaching (JALT) International Conference. After the forum, I asked her if she would be willing to tell her story for this project and we spent an evening in a cafe recording and chatting. I sent Renata the text of her story as soon as I had finished transcribing it. Subsequently, Renata returned the text with several amendments, which served to anonymise some of the people she mentioned as well as to further 'clean up' the text by removing discourse markers and grammatical infelicities. This is the version of the story that Renata approved.

Renata's Story

I remember when I was a teenager I didn't like studying and I never dreamt of becoming a teacher. Although as a kid I enjoyed acting like a teacher because of the blackboard and the chalk. I thought teaching would never be my profession. I went to an all-girls private Catholic school from kindergarten to high school. I was a stubborn and curious student so I kept on asking questions. When I went to the University of the Philippines I was exposed to different kinds of people. I had some free time and my friend encouraged me to do tutoring. So I thought I would do that and I kind of enjoyed it.

My major was theater and I belonged to the Department of Speech Communication and Theatre Arts. When I was finishing my dissertation, I started working for television but when I graduated I felt like I couldn't just do media. First, the money wasn't enough and second, it was tiring and exhausting. I was producing shows and developing ideas for popular TV shows. First I worked for a big TV company, then after that I went on to produce travel shows, magazine shows. I did everything: producing, directing, writing. Someone suggested, why don't I go back to teach drama at my high school alma mater? They were looking for a part-time teacher. I thought why not, because that was my passion since high school. So I was in media and I was teaching drama.

My parents were also encouraging me to study here in Japan. They said why don't you apply for this scholarship? My sister was already doing that. But I had a partner then and I hesitated. But finally I applied, and surprisingly I was able to get a scholarship to do my masters at N University. I enjoyed teaching, it was just like playing, it was drama. When I was doing my masters, I was not sure if I wanted to pursue a career in the academe. My professor was asking if I wanted to pursue a PhD, but at that time I couldn't see myself in academe. I missed doing jobs in film. I also had an apprenticeship in cinematography. I had this idea that I could do teaching and media, but I had to choose one.

When I was a student at N University, I heard from other Filipino students that I could teach English part time. So in a way, that helped my life in Japan. Not just because of the money, but I met my first Japanese friends in that school. Most of them have lived abroad so they're not the typical, traditional Japanese. They helped me with Japanese language and culture as well. It was a good experience. After I finished my masters, I went back home and joined a Catholic private university, not as an English teacher but in the Japanese Studies program. I was teaching Japanese gender, Japanese cinema. And that's when I felt that I was becoming part of the academe.

Then Japan was calling me back because of my residence visa. I'm partly Japanese. So I had to return, and this time I came to Tokyo. My grandfather's hometown is in Yamaguchi-ken, but I never met him because he died during the war. I started all over again in Tokyo, I didn't know anyone. I worked at an eikaiwa. But I wanted more, I really wanted to teach at university. It was easy to get a job at an eikaiwa. I told them I had experience working at the university. They were outsourcing so I told them I want to teach at university if you're going to outsource teachers. At first when you're starting you want to follow their teaching methods, but it's all about just getting the hang of it. Anyone can teach. I think they are hiring anyone. If you have experience in teaching, then good, but if not, then they will train you. If you have so many lessons a day, you can hone your teaching skill.

Then I joined a private university, teaching full time. After a year, I realised I need a PhD. So I went back to school, while teaching full time. It's also interesting because it's a different kind of atmosphere. Sociologists are different, we're working with anthropologists as well. They have different research methods. Where I teach, I'm working with people who are in education, applied linguistics, linguistics, TESOL, it's also a different way of analysing data.

In my classes, I try to use only English, even if the beginners are having a very hard time. I'm full-time and I know I can handle it, so I get those students. I try as much as possible not to use Japanese at all. If I use Japanese, they will speak to me in Japanese. I could use written Japanese, but for explaining instructions, it's always been my policy to use just English. I do it because I think it works.

Our centre is not only hiring native speakers but also non-native speakers. We believe that students will have more opportunities in the future to talk to non-native speakers. They'll be doing business in Asia. Am I a native speaker? I don't want labels actually. I think it's a very Japanese way of thinking. But for people who are not linguists but just use the language, we don't think about it. In the Philippines, some Filipinos criticise other Filipinos' English accent. It's not actually the grammar, it's the pronunciation, how you write. Among the Filipinos, within Filipino English, there are categories. So where do you put the native speaker? I don't see it anymore. When I studied English, it was all American English, we weren't exposed to British English. Those people who lived abroad, like my relatives, sometimes they become Americanized. Suddenly they couldn't speak Filipino anymore. How can you forget your mother tongue? They could understand but they don't want to speak the language. That's so sad.

I like working with a diverse faculty. If I were a student I would like that, getting used to all different kinds of English, being aware of different cultures and different backgrounds. I experienced that at one of the longest running eikaiwa companies, and not just educational background, but really extreme backgrounds. There were older people who started working there at that time when they weren't hiring non-native speakers. So for them, seeing non-native speakers being hired, it's a whole new way of thinking.

I didn't feel there was any resentment toward me. Actually, I don't care. If you're not into teaching, you could get affected. Not just English teaching, but if you don't enjoy teaching itself, that would bother you a lot.

I try to make my classes fun. Ideally, I want my students to have more interaction, so I invite foreign students, guest speakers, non-native or native speaker. Sometimes I do drama workshop. I invite a theatre artist from the Philippines and we do a one-day workshop. We do a lot of film-showing, we watch videos. I don't just use a textbook. I do use one because they bought it, but I try not to focus on the textbook. I try to encourage debate and discussion, I think that's very important, because they lack that. Whether they study abroad or whether they graduate, they need to think for themselves. Because I'm also a sociologist, I expose them to different kinds of topics, because they need to know that, especially about gender. Maybe in general, Japanese young people nowadays don't care about politics. They just don't care, and that's sad, right? Because they're the next generation. Compared to my country, we were starting demos, we were aware, so it's kind of sad. It's not just where I teach but other universities too. It's a Japanese trend. So I try to put political issues in my class too. I don't know if it's ignorance or indifference, it could be both. They don't even vote.

I let them discuss in Japanese. I give them time to translate it. We encourage them to use Japanese, do code-switching. I heard at other schools, it's English only. I don't want that. So I let them speak Japanese. Writing is a lot of work. They're using those software application translation softwares, machine translation, so there's a tendency for them to plagiarise. Writing is really difficult. There should be a special class, focusing on writing. But our centre covers all skills, listening, speaking, reading, writing. English is a requirement, all students at H University have to take English. If you are an English major, you also have to take it. I think they have the policy of Lingua Franca because of O-sensei. There were already other departments that had an English program. But then the centre was conceptualised by O-sensei. There is Tourism English program. There's also English Education but our Centre of English as a Lingua Franca, CELF is different.

I found out about FETJ through another Filipino at the eikaiwa who became a leader of FETJ. He knew about my research and I asked him if I could gather data. When we met, they said, 'Why don't you give a talk?' and then at that event I conducted my survey. Before that I had a presentation at Kanda University in 2013. There was this guy from a publishing company, he listened to my presentation and he told me, 'You could get in touch with FETJ'. He said, 'They're kind of aggressive, those Filipinos'. The image of FETJ for me, they also do volunteer work, which is good. But they're not just helping other Filipinos, they do some outreach programs too. So I thought it's a support group for Filipinos who just came to Japan. It was a challenge for me to get data from FETJ because there's a hierarchy, you know. I got in touch with someone, but I didn't know she was the top person, and then I went to other people, and I don't think they liked that. If you're a researcher, it's not that easy to get in. Even if you are a Filipino. So that was my last contact with them.

What strikes me in Renata's story is that being an English teacher is not something that she aspired to from childhood (unlike most of the other narrators), although teaching is something she has done throughout her career, both as a temporary means to make or subsidise her living and as a point along the road to an academic career. The starting point of her career history resembles Aurora's in that both women entered the media straight after obtaining their bachelor's degree in the Philippines, Aurora as a television broadcaster and Renata as a producer. However, Renata's transition from the media into an academic career is facilitated by a number of factors that are absent or different in Aurora's story, such as her status as a single woman, as a Japanese descendant (she is *sansei*, like Sampaguita) and as a graduate of the most prestigious university in the Philippines and, subsequently, of a high-ranked national university in Japan. Her experience is also different because she started to work full time in Japan in 2014, more than 20 years after Aurora first started working as a teacher for Shogakan, a period of gradual change in attitudes towards Filipinos in Japan.

Prejudice and pride are harder to detect in Renata's story. She denies that there was any prejudice towards her as a Filipino by the *eikaiwa* company that hired her ('*Anyone can teach. I think they are hiring anyone*'), although she is aware that this was not the case in the past. On reflection, she admits that some native English teachers may have felt threatened by the change, but claims that she was unaware of, or at least unconcerned about any possible negative feeling towards her at the *eikaiwa*. In her present job at the Centre for English as a Lingua Franca at H University, her national identity is, if anything, an asset, contributing to the diversity of the teaching faculty. If there is any prejudice towards her in the story, it is perhaps in the account she gives of her contact with FETJ. Although she does not explain what happened in any detail, it seems that her request to conduct research on FETJ members generated resentment because of some unspoken protocol in seeking permission of which she was unaware. Renata claims that the group's resistance to her request was because she was a 'researcher'. I did not question Renata's claim, but it conflicts with my own experience with FETJ. Were they more resistant to Renata *because* she is Filipino? And more amenable to me *because* I am British?

Prejudice and pride are not emotions that feature in any clear way in Renata's story. She brings an academic detachment, and a sociologist's eye, to her discussion of linguistic identity ('*Among the Filipinos, within Filipino English, there are categories*'). Renata rejects the 'native-speaker label', denigrating it as 'a very Japanese way of thinking' or something that only 'linguists' care about. Perhaps Renata's privileged position (Appleby, 2016) not only in the Philippines, but also in Japanese society, inoculates her from (and hence makes her blind to) the prejudice that is reportedly felt by many other Filipinos who come to Japan. In any case, she works in a context where traditional labels are discarded and a diversity of Englishes is preferred.

Renata may not express pride, *per se*, but she does voice her opinions, sometimes quite emotively, about various issues relating to identity. She thinks it is 'sad', for example, that Filipinos who move to America, like some of her relatives, lose their Filipino languages. Similarly, it's sad that Japanese students seem to be ignorant about or indifferent to politics, unlike students in the Philippines, who are much more aware and active, in her opinion. Accordingly, she takes action to try to change her students by injecting political issues into her English teaching. Clearly, Renata has strong views on many issues, including on English language teaching as a practice and as a professional identity, and these will be examined later in this chapter.

I now turn to Carmela's story. I met Carmela through Renata who introduced her to me as a possible collaborator, at the JALT conference forum that I previously mentioned. Carmela had moved to Tokyo from Gifu on the Japan Sea coast two years previously, but, as she explains in her story, had plans to move back to Gifu the following year. We met in central Tokyo close to the university where she was working, and found a quiet corner in a cafe to record Carmela's story. The longest recording by far, this version, which Carmela amended for reasons similar to Renata's, has been abridged, but at over 3000 words, it is at least twice as long as any of the other narratives. It is presented here without any further abridgement or amendment to respect the narrator's telling of it.

Carmela's Story

Except for my first year or two in elementary, all my education was in public school. In high school, I realised that I was very much interested in science and in my second year I won a quiz in a big provincial competition, the first person in my school to win that award. I wanted to be doctor, but my father told me that if I went to medical school, there wouldn't be enough money to put my younger siblings through university. So I studied agriculture, major in animal sciences and minor in business studies, at the university in the nearby island. I thought that with business studies, I'd also be able to help my father later on.

I finished the degree there, graduating cum laude, *and was employed right away by the ministry to work with farmers. I enjoyed the work, but I realised that I wanted to be back in school. So I went back to college to do an MBA. But I was still looking for what I could do so during the course I decided to get a teachers licence with the idea that I would teach business or agricultural sciences. When I told my father I wanted to change to a private university to get a teachers licence, he was shocked but said OK, as I only needed to study for one semester to get the credits I needed for the license. So I got my license and I applied to teach in the provincial high school in Iloilo. It's a huge school, with a wide range of students, sectioned into 18 groups, so they had the best and the worst. I had a walk-in interview and the principal accepted me. I started teaching electives in agricultural science and I did projects like creating a poultry farm and a greenhouse. The principal loved what I was doing. She really liked me, even called me her daughter-in-law! I did really well in that school for three years. I also enrolled in a masters of science in education program with major in biological science and minor in school administration, transferring my credits from the MBA, and that was helpful for getting promotion as a teacher in the school.*

Then an announcement came out for people to teach in a refugee camp in Bataan. I had taken English courses myself at university, and I taught my subjects in English, but I had no experience of teaching English. But I decided to apply and was accepted. My principal was so upset, she said 'How can you go? You are our favourite!' She made me promise to come back after one year. So I went, and I loved working in the camp. It was run by NGOs under the UNHCR and had about 24,000 refugees from Vietnam, Laos and Cambodia. Because of the influx of refugees, they hired 104 at that time, though I was the only one from my island. We had to speak Tagalog, but I wished I could speak Hiligaynon sometimes. Anyway, I was teaching adults there and that was where my career in language teaching started.

Language teaching training was completely different to what I had done before. I really enjoyed team-building activities and the experience of using communicative language teaching. These refugees needed language and they needed confidence. They would be applying for settlement in the US or Australia and they had to pass an interview, so it was very important, very intense. The camp was on top of a mountain and we would work without a break for six weeks and then rest for two weeks. During that time, we could not play, and it was too much for many of the teachers. But the work here really moulded my ideas about what I wanted to do.

When the budget for the UNHCR program was cut, I moved to the secondary camp nearby where refugees who had not succeeded in getting to the US or Australia were applying for settlement in European countries. Here I was working in a supervisory role, working with Vietnamese translators, and it was tough. In this camp I was teaching chemistry to kids. We tried to emulate the school system of the countries they would be going to, so all the classes were in English. Working as an administrator, I was able to go to meetings with UNHCR and I could understand what was going on at a higher level, so I knew they were moving their focus to Rwanda and would cut the budget for the program in the Philippines.

So I looked around and saw that there was an opening for a teacher in Cambodia and applied. However, I got a reply saying they had already accepted someone who was based in Cambodia, but they would pass my resume onto another agency. So I stopped thinking about that. At the same time, I learned that, because of the cuts, two new teachers would have to be laid off. Because I was supervising and teaching, I decided to barter my jobs for theirs, since they both had families and needed the work more than me. I resigned and went back home. On my way, I stopped in Manila where I bought a rabbit for my brother. A little boy came up to me and wanted to play with the rabbit and I started talking to his parents. They were British and it turned out their company had to start a project in Cambodia. They gave me the address of their office in Manila and said I could pass my resume to them there. I had just enough time to do that before catching the boat back to my island. Three weeks later I received a telegram: come to Manila for an interview. The interviewer brought out the resume that I had given the British couple and then another resume that I had sent from the refugee camp and had forgotten about. So that was how I came to work in Cambodia.

The Cambodian project was for a Buddhist NGO based in Japan. The classes were juku style: university students came from 6 am to 8.30, and then classes in the afternoon from 4.30 to 6. There were no materials. My colleague from Bataan gave me a big box of materials and said copy whatever you want. That helped a lot. I couldn't afford to buy books, and we didn't have a library. I was always at the British Council; that was the only place I could get books. There was no Internet, it came about two years later. The experience in Cambodia made me more interested in language. The British Council gave training to locals and I sometimes attended that. We worked for the Ministry of Education and we had to connect with the only other language programs in the country. We also went to Thailand for materials and Thai TESOL. Our building was inside University of Phnom Penh. Many of the students were professionals: doctors, engineers, stewardesses. So my experience in the camp really helped. It was communicative English, not grammar – that's not really my forte – my colleague and I worked hard with an Australian lady who was running the foreign language resource at the university. We were in this big building, it's still there. Working in that environment, it's working and living with those people and hearing their stories, about the Pol Pot time, my goodness. These were stories I heard in the camp too. It was still unstable in Cambodia, we heard gunshots all the time in the first year. Very tough. We had curfew, I had to be home by 6 pm. After two years the situation became more stable. But there were still so many robberies. You would lose your car as soon as you parked it. But I loved the work and the students were hungry for English. The private English jukus, you'd see an eight-year old boy with grown working men, you will cry to see it. And you can imagine how rich the teacher was.

I got married in my second year. We met in the Philippines. He was my co-worker and attended my class there. He tried to get a job in Cambodia when he realised I was there. We moved to Japan in 1996, after *the Kobe earthquake. I realised that I wouldn't have a job when I moved there, so I asked my office, instead of sending me to Thai TESOL, send me to JALT. At the JALT conference I met a couple of colleagues from the refugee camp who had moved to Japan and had good stable work. They said they like it but warned me not to be disappointed or discouraged by the 'native speaker syndrome'. My Filipino colleague said he had been through all this.*

When I first came, I had no choice but to stay in the house with my mother-in-law. My sister-in-law said, 'I can be your student', so she brought two friends and we squeezed into the small room. Then my mother in the Philippines got sick, and I went back. When I returned, my husband had got us a bigger apartment and when I got back at the end of the summer, I made flyers and found some students. By November I had 31 students. Most were adults, and there were about six children. So for nine years I was doing that, and I also got a job at the elementary school in 2000 when the ministry started introducing English. I had to do the curriculum because they did not have one. I went to the orientation and said, 'This is something that I know how to do'. Then I was assigned to two other schools, so I was going to three schools. I told the school I could only teach first and second period, and then I would teach after that at home. My daughter was at kindergarten, and I needed to be there for her. And I would teach adults at night. So I did that for many years. I helped the teachers develop their curriculum and I was asked to train the teachers, though it was hard for them. They don't have the language, so everything was left for me. The head teacher of English was very good at teaching in English. Running the programme, they felt that they had to be in control. But I told them that they would be moving around and then the next teachers would not know what to do. So he came up with all the books I recommended, and we chose the activities, the songs we liked, and the schools started to use them. Most schools have warm-up songs for the morning and for the afternoon.

After I taught in elementary school, once a month I was asked to visit the kindergarten. And this led me to do a part-time job in the college. They said, 'Why don't you teach English to the primary education college students?' That is where I was able to use the books on communicative teaching that I'd been using with adult students in my house. So I was working at the college part time, and the kindergarten which was under the same umbrella. And then the elementary schools and teaching at home. I could do that because my husband was away, so I was juggling everything. My husband was working in Kansai and he would send his laundry by takyubin [delivery company]. *For a few years it was like that.*

When my daughter entered elementary school, I decided to apply for a full-time job. Well, I applied for the Board of Education job in a nearby city, me and Jane and another American. But they need only one, so they took Jane. I went to the interview to see what it was like. I already knew how to do this. Moreover, I could understand that Wendy would be taken because she is American and maybe she is really good. I was probably the first non-native teacher to apply for the local city Board of Education schools. Anyway, I couldn't do it because of my daughter. The following year, they called me for an interview. I did not hesitate. I had enough experience in elementary school. I thought I can't let this opportunity go. The year before the panel took a lot, about seven people. But this year, there were only a few. And I was taken. But I had to stop the college and the kindergarten and the students in the house. The year before that, I had started my masters at UTS, Sydney. I was already in the middle of that. So my purpose of getting into a full-time job was to have stable money to finish my school. So that is how I juggled everything.

Believe me, I'm amazed at my energy. The one thing I really regret was I was not able to go home to the Philippines. In December I was asked if I would go back to the college. The sound of research, the stability was really attractive. But I could not decide. The local city Board of Education wanted me to stay and to run a summer camp, where I met Mrs K, a legend among teachers. We worked together and I learned a lot. There were a lot of teachers working on different activities, cultural activities, we did one with an Olympic theme. We could see that there were some teachers who were not committed to teaching, who were just doing it for the money. But we in the community see that it is important. I really feel that. I really commit to the students. So finally, I thought that the Board of Education job, you don't grow, you only give. And I thought it was high time for me to learn more, to do research.

So I'm working at the college when 2012 December I received a notice that my contract will finish in March the following year and I may not be able to renew. It was shocking, so I asked the president, 'Did I do anything wrong?' 'No, but' she said 'please just wait, don't make any decisions'. But I still thought maybe I did something wrong, so I looked for other jobs and I quietly asked the pastor for a reference to a Christian school. So I sent only to Y University, and they invited me to an interview and demo, and said I could choose presentation class or writing class. The day of my interview, I had class before in the evening and I stayed in my office and prepared material for a demonstration of a presentation class. I paid for a hotel only 5000 yen, a really smelly hotel. I went to the interview and I enjoyed it. I walked around the campus and thought I really wanted to go there. I got the job, and when I told my college, the vice president really sulked, but it was their fault, they did not make the position clear. So the president said 'OK, you can go, but maybe when you have finished you can come back'. So I went to Y University and it was a good move. Then in 2015 December, I got a mail from my old college saying they were having a meeting, so I went and found out that they are creating a new education department in 2017. They asked me to submit my resume and all these papers, so they could submit to the

Monbusho. Then July and another set of papers arrived. If you consider this, you have to fill this out. I received a call in September and then October I had to decide. I'd seen teachers who had completed the five-year contract at Y University fail to get a full-time job and other teachers left before they finished the contract. So I decided to go back. I don't know what's god's plan.

I heard about FETJ through JALT when I was Gifu chapter president. FETJ wanted to join the national membership so, when they had a seminar in Nagoya, I decided to go. I brought along two friends who were aspiring teachers. There was some trouble at the start. A foreign guy from Shiga tried to get in, but they said it was only for Filipinos. How many times I asked them to answer my emails, Facebook messages. But in the end we were all gathered in a community centre. They were doing an activity using a CD, and they couldn't figure it out, but I knew the CD well and I could prompt them – it's number 7. So they wanted to know who I was, and they identified me as someone who knows how to do this. I handed in my name tag, my meishi *(business card), and the president ran after me, 'Where is this school? How did you get this job?' I said, 'OK, just reach me', but he never contacted me. I said, 'Whatever you need, probably you need help, you can ask me'. So I thought maybe they have other resources.*

I met Aurora at one of Marco's events in Gifu, and then I met the president of the FETJ Gifu chapter. They seem to be stable, they have their teacher guidelines. But so many teachers need to go beyond what they are doing. With the development of English in Japan, they really have to go on training seminars. Filipinos are hesitant to work alongside other foreign nationals. They put themselves in a secluded situation where they ask foreign trainers to train them, and that is beneficial because they have control of their own group. And the trainer is just there as the resource. They have the flexibility of getting motivation of each other and being a strong community. For them, they have no real training of language teaching and they are still developing their career in that direction. Otherwise, they need a tangible diploma to prove they can teach. It's a good stepping-stone for them. They can develop confidence. But somehow, FETJ has responsibility to also let these people who are getting into advanced stage to do training. Somehow that can elevate the status of many Filipinos. I think that the past image of Filipinos is fading. It's amazing, I think the impact of FETJ has been great.

The tone of Carmela's narrative is markedly different from Renata's narrative. Her high-octane, fast-moving career history is matched by the highly emotive language with which she describes it. Closer in age to Aurora (and to me), Carmela came to Japan in the mid-1990s, when negative stereotypes about Filipinos were still relatively common. Nevertheless, where she encounters prejudice, it is, in her view, because of her identity as a 'non-native English speaker' more than because of her national identity as a Filipino. Before she moves to Japan, she attends a JALT conference and is warned by Filipino colleagues from the refugee camp in Bataan who had since relocated to Japan not to be '*disappointed or discouraged by the "native speaker syndrome"*'. Later, when she applies for a job with the board of education, she is unsurprised when an American woman is hired instead of her, and more surprised when the board contacts her the following year to ask her to come again for interview.

There is plenty of pride in Carmela's story. From the time she was a high school student and was the first person in her school to win an important prize in a provincial competition for science onwards, Carmela documents a series of successes in her developing career: her employment with the Ministry of Agriculture, the large provincial high school in Iloilo, her switch to English teaching at the refugee camp in Bataan and subsequent promotion to supervisor. In Japan, she starts taking private students while her daughter is a baby, and quickly acquires a large number of students. In quick succession, she is hired to teach in an elementary school and then at a college training Japanese to teach English in elementary school, she starts a distance master's degree and is then hired by a board of education. No wonder she is 'amazed' at her own energy. Carmela does not hesitate to promote her own expertise, not out of vanity, but because she believes she has know-how and experience that will be of use to the Japanese elementary schools that are introducing English for the first time. When she has setbacks in her career, she remains sanguine about the causes and about her future prospects. Serendipity also plays a role in Carmela's story: aware that funding for the refugee camp English teaching programme will be stopped, she resigns so that two other teachers can stay. Then, on her way home in Manila, she happens to meet a British couple involved in a non-governmental organisation (NGO) teaching programme in Cambodia to which she had applied, but received no response. There is also a certain degree of fatalism in Carmela's story ('*what's god's plan for me?*'), which suggests that she has been willing to risk her own security and well-being for a greater good – a different kind of altruism to that which we have seen in the stories of the FETJ teachers.

Unlike the FETJ members, whose self-positioning in the narratives was to a large extent influenced by the research purpose that I told them and the context in which the interviews were conducted, Renata and Carmela were not members of FETJ and their teacher identity, as such, is more open to question. Absent from their narratives is any suggestion that their identity as *Filipinos* was detrimental to their professional lives. Carmela does appear to take for granted the fact that she was passed over for a job with a board of education in favour of a rival candidate who was American, but this can be explained by her earlier claim that fellow Filipinos had warned of the 'native-speaker syndrome' in Japan.

Similarly, Renata implies that some native-speaker teachers at the *eikaiwa* might have a negative attitude towards non-native teachers, but states firmly that she did not feel such 'resentment' and that it would not have affected her even if there had been. Since FETJ is not a significant factor in their stories, are there other groups or social identity categories that are significant?

Self-Categorisation Analysis

One way to explore this question is from a social identity perspective (Abrams & Hogg, 1990; Markus & Kitayama, 1991; Tajfel & Turner, 1979), which holds that we define ourselves in terms of our relationships to others as well as to social groups. In our interaction with others, which would include here narration of our life stories, we frequently classify ourselves and other people into social categories, and, in doing so, we associate certain 'relevant' attributes with the categories we invoke (Antaki & Widdicombe, 1998), including rights, entitlements, obligations, knowledge, attributes and competencies (Hester & Eglin, 1997: 5, cited in Gray & Morton, 2018: 80). The identities we ascribe to ourselves and others are indexical and occasioned. In other words, they are called into being within and by specific contexts. They are purposeful, consequential and observable (Antaki & Widdicombe, 1998). Membership categorisation is also an evaluative stance, in which 'maintenance of social identity boundaries is not just dependent on "knowing" the status of one's own category membership, but upon accomplishing this membership through the interactional work of hierarchical categorisations' (Nilan, 1995).

In their review of research and theory of the social self, Brewer and Gardner (1996) propose that the personal (*I*), relational (*we*) and collective (*we*) levels of self-definition represent distinct forms of self-representation. Both relational and collective levels of self-definition are extensions of the social self. However, relational self-definition denotes personal bonds (e.g. family, colleagues, students), whereas collective self-definition denotes affiliation with larger, impersonal social categories, such as national identity (e.g. Filipino, Japanese or American) or linguistic identity (e.g. native, non-native speaker), among others. Although membership categories are sometimes merely implied, they are often signalled explicitly through the choice of pronouns. Lexical choice has been used to analyse professional identity in novice language teachers (Pavlenko, 2003) and pronoun choice specifically was the focus of a study of American schoolchildren's talk about Japan by Inokuchi and Nozaki (2005). Here, I examine the personal pronouns that Renata and Carmela employ in their narratives, with a particular focus on the relational and collective *we* pronouns, as a way of gaining insight into the membership categories they invoke, and hence their teacher identities.

Analysis of Personal Pronoun Use

A simple search of the transcripts yields the numerical details of pronoun use by Renata and Carmela, shown in Table 6.1.

Table 6.1 Frequency of personal pronoun use in Renata's and Carmela's narratives

Pronoun	Renata	Carmela
I	125	184
We (relational)	6	20
We (collective)	5	1

The ratio of singular to plural personal pronoun use is slightly narrower in the case of Carmela (Renata 1:11; Carmela 1:8), but what is most striking in Table 6.1 is the difference in the relative use of the relational compared with the collective *we*, with Renata using the collective form (5) almost as often as the relational form (6) and Carmela using the collective form only once, compared with 20 uses of the relational form.

Let us examine their respective uses of the collective *we* more closely. Table 6.2 lists the incidences of the collective *we* that occur in Renata's narrative.

Table 6.2 Renata's use of the collective **we**

(1) *'Sociologists are different, we're working with anthropologists as well'*
(2) *'But for people who are not linguists but just use the language, we don't think about it'*
(3) *'When I studied English, it was all American English, we weren't exposed to British English'*
(4) *'Compared to my country, we were starting demos, we were aware'* (2)

Renata's use of the collective *we* points to two distinct membership categories: in (1) and (2), Renata categorises herself as a sociologist, not a linguist. Certainly, there are grounds for this self-categorisation: Renata is enrolled in a PhD programme as a sociologist. But at the same time, she could have chosen to represent herself differently, as her background was in drama and media and her full-time job is as an English language teacher at a Japanese university. Affiliating herself with sociologists, she is able to distance herself from, and thus resist the native/non-native controversy. 'We don't think about it', she asserts, unlike 'linguists' and 'Japanese'. In (3), she speaks as a Filipino national, defining her own English as 'American' (compared with my British accent?), and in (4), Filipino identity is used as a foil to highlight the contrasting characteristic of Japanese students as apolitical and unaware. As with the sociologist self-ascription, here Renata's self-categorisation as a Filipino lends weight to her claimed identity as an English speaker (with an American accent) and as a politically aware person.

Now let us examine the single use of the collective *we* in Carmela's narrative (Table 6.3).

Table 6.3 Carmela's use of the collective *we*

(1) *'We in the community see that it is important'*

In her narrative, Carmela, in contrast with Renata, employs the collective *we* only once. In all other 20 instances, *we* is used in a relational sense to refer to herself and other specific people as subjects of actions that she describes. Indeed, in the one example of the collective *we*, it is worth examining the context in which this statement appears:

> *The local city Board of Education wanted me to stay and to run a summer camp, where I met Mrs K, a legend among teachers. We worked together and I learned a lot. There were a lot of teachers working on different activities, cultural activities, we did one with an Olympic theme. We could see that there were some teachers who were not committed to teaching, who were just doing it for the money. **But we in the community see that it is important.** I really feel that. I really commit to the students.*

From the theoretical perspectives of narrative that I discussed earlier (Labov & Waletzky, 1967; Sacks, 1974), this constitutes a complete narrative within the larger career history. The narrative has a subject (Carmela met the legendary Mrs K at a summer camp), an orientation (they worked together and Carmela learned a lot), a complication (some teachers were not committed to teaching and were just doing it for the money) and a resolution-coda ('we in the community' see that it is important to be committed to teaching). Notably, this mini-narrative contains the strongest assertion of Carmela's feeling about being a teacher. Her commitment to her students is also a commitment to the community in which she lives. There is no sense here that she does not imagine herself as fully belonging to this community. Her ethnic or national identity as a Filipino does not figure in any way in her narrative.

Outsiders' Representation of FETJ

Renata and Carmela are not members of FETJ and have pursued careers in and around English language teaching without any assistance from that group. Both, however, have had some contact with FETJ, and it is thus worth looking at their representation of the group and their own relationship, as this can provide some insight into how the identity politics that I have discussed in earlier chapters can be viewed by people who are not beneficiaries of it and who may hold different and critical views about it.

First of all, Renata relates how she wanted to gain access to FETJ as a 'researcher', invoking again the self-categorisation of 'sociologist' that she had constructed earlier. Indeed, this 'researcher' category proves to be crucial to the significance of this story-within-a-story, since it is this identity that proves, in her view, to be the 'relevant' (Edwards, 1998) thing about her for FETJ, over and above her identity as a fellow Filipino ('*If you're a researcher, it's not that easy to get in. Even if you are a Filipino*'). Renata's depiction of FETJ is rife with contradictions. Although the gist of her story about her encounter with the group is largely negative, she claims she has a positive image of the group because of their volunteer work, their outreach programmes and their support for Filipinos new to Japan. However, the picture she conveys of the group is quite negative. She cites a publisher she met at a conference ('*They're kind of aggressive, those Filipinos*'), and although she does not go into much detail, she seems to have encountered, or perhaps been the cause of, some bad feeling because she was unaware of the group's hierarchy and hence of the right way to approach them with her request to conduct a survey at one of their meetings.

Carmela's picture of FETJ, like Renata's, is quite contradictory, and her portrayal of the group is very much from the perspective of an outsider. To begin with, Carmela mentions that she first heard about FETJ in her capacity as president of a regional chapter of JALT. Right away, she appears to cast FETJ in a subaltern category compared with the much larger and established JALT organisation. (In fact, FETJ did become an associate member of JALT.) What she chooses to describe of the event is the problems: the 'trouble at the start' when 'a foreign guy' was denied entry; the difficulty she had in getting a response to her efforts to contact the group; and the problem the presenter had with the CD she was using. Carmela casts herself as someone who is more knowledgeable (she prompts the presenter with the correct song on the CD) and more professional (she objects to communication delays but offers to help and proffers her business card as she leaves). She concedes that FETJ has become a stable group with their teacher guidelines and she ends by saying that 'the impact of FETJ has been great'. However, she claims that what the group is doing is too limited ('*they need to go beyond what they are doing. They really have to go on training seminars*'). For Carmela, FETJ's main issue is one of control. As she explains:

> *Filipinos are hesitant to work alongside other foreign nationals. They put themselves in secluded situation where they ask foreign trainers to train them, and that is beneficial because they have control of their own group. And the trainer is just there as the resource.*

This, in my view, is a rather inaccurate picture of the work of FETJ, whose main activity consists, as we have seen, of teacher training novice and more experienced teachers, although it is certainly true that guest presenters, both foreign and Filipino, are invited to events. Perhaps Carmela resents the fact that the Gifu chapter of FETJ did not invite her to participate, afraid that her knowledge and experience would give her too much influence.

Both Renata and Carmela trace successful careers as English teachers (although Renata prefers to present herself as a sociologist who happens to teach English). The fact that they come from the Philippines has little relevance to their teacher identity, as they represent it. For Renata, her Filipino identity is an asset, even in the *eikaiwa* where in the past non-Inner-Circle English teachers would have been excluded, but particularly in her current job in the Centre of English as a Lingua Franca at H University. Various factors can explain Renata's success and her relative ease in being hired for English teaching positions: her social class as a graduate both of the Philippine's most prestigious university and a high-ranking Japanese graduate school, her Japanese *sansei* identity and her Japanese language proficiency, and it is these attributes that would appear to outweigh any need for professional English teaching qualifications. In Carmela's case, her Filipino identity is simply not relevant. Through her career narrative, she presents an image of an international, or transnational person (De Fina & Perrino, 2013; Duff, 2015), a teacher who has taught in a range of institutions in different countries, a teacher who is highly qualified, highly experienced and highly committed to her students. Both Renata and Carmela applaud FETJ's work and its contribution to raising the status of Filipinos in Japan, but the equivocations they raise at the end of their narratives imply that they believe that there is no longer any need to save Filipinos from social stigma.

7 Conclusions

I started this book with the assertion that identity matters. It matters to everyone, but it matters particularly to language teachers, because we work at the interface between and across languages and cultures; our identities are 'on show' to learners and the people who hire us as part of our pedagogical repertoire (Morgan, 2004). And it matters even more to Filipino English teachers working in Japan, because their potential and legitimacy to teach English has in the past been dismissed for reasons that include 'native-speakerism' and prejudice against Filipinos, particularly Filipino women who have been denigrated as '*japayuki*'.

I began by presenting a critique of the post-structuralist theories of identity whose emphasis on discourse fails to account for the real social, economic and affective consequences of our identity, consequences that can be positive as well as negative. As an alternative explanation, I have looked to theories of identity as recognition, in which recognition is viewed as the precondition for ontological security and social justice. In contrast with a post-structuralist assumption that notions of 'good' and 'right' and 'just' are ideological, I argue, following Honneth (1995, 2012), that such moral evaluations relate to real conditions that evoke real and deeply felt emotions, in particular prejudice and pride. I have attempted to explain the *mis*recognition of Filipinos in Japan within a historical context, and I have presented the career histories of successful Filipino English teachers to show how and where they feel that they are recognised for their identity as English teachers. The seven career narratives by members of Filipino English Teacher in Japan (FETJ) speak for themselves as inspiring accounts of Filipinos becoming English teachers and helping others in the same venture. They also provide a way in to commentary on and critique of various aspects of language teacher identity: identity as self-investment versus identity as recognition; the formation and role of language teacher associations (LTAs); and what the notions of 'career' and 'work' might mean for English language teachers. The final two narratives by Filipino teachers, who are not members of FETJ, provide data for an analysis of pronoun choice in self-representation. The accounts by these two outsiders serve to give balance to the picture of

Filipinos in Japan as well as to explore different kinds of teacher identity among Filipinos in that country.

Writing this book has led me to think deeply and critically about current theories of identity and the language that applied linguists use to talk about it. While my overall aim has been to propose an alternative epistemology for thinking about identity, one that emphasises recognition rather than discourse, I have also taken a critical stance on various other concepts that are generally viewed as unproblematic in relation to teacher identity. Now, in this concluding chapter, and in light of all nine narratives, I would like to reflect on four of these – three theoretical and one methodological – in which I have departed from the current conventional practice or focus in teacher identity research. These are identity politics, identity metaphors, teacher communities and narrative. What are the implications of a recognition approach for these concepts and what new directions for research on teacher identity might be taken?

Identity Politics: Widening the Research Horizon

A focus on the political dimension of language teacher identity has become increasingly prominent in studies that explore marginalised identities, such as race, ethnicity, gender, sexuality, colonialism and social class, in an occupation that is itself often regarded as marginalised in the context of formal education (Linville & Whiting, 2019). It is indeed largely thanks to studies such as these that the marginalisation of these identities has been brought to our attention. But marginalisation itself is a slippery concept. 'Power is everywhere', Foucault (1988: 63) proclaims, and it 'comes from everywhere'. Until relatively recently, Filipinos were marginalised in Japan in the sense that few of them were accepted as legitimate English teachers. But then being an English teacher was not something to which many Filipinos aspired. Accepting a drop in social status as economic migrants to Japan may have been a reasonable exchange for the opportunity to earn far more than would be possible at home and for the opportunity to provide help and encouragement to newcomers. Foucault used the term *power/knowledge* to signify that 'power is constituted through accepted forms of knowledge, scientific understanding and "truth": "Truth" is a thing of this world: it is produced only by virtue of multiple forms of constraint' (Foucault, cited in Rabinow, 1991). But 'constraint' is not the only way that 'truth' is produced. As I have sought to argue and illustrate with the narratives in this book, 'recognition' is a form of liberation. Filipinos should not have to be limited to working in bars or factories in Japan, or any other country. If they speak English, why should they not have every right to become English language teachers, or any other occupation that they desire? In fact, as I have sought to illustrate by the sequencing of the narratives, Filipinos have been very successful in moving into the field of English language teaching in Japan, helped in no small measure by FETJ and other Filipino organisations and social networks. Just as certain national groups have come to dominate particular occupations in particular areas, such as the Pakistani corner shops in the United Kingdom of the 1970s and 1980s, or Vietnamese nail salons in present-day California (Piller, 2012), will English teaching become the stereotypical occupation for Filipinos in Japan?

Recent thinking about language teacher identity has highlighted the problem of structure and agency. Structure is generally seen as a bad thing, a constraint on teacher's autonomy. Phil Benson (2016: 20) states that, 'Identity signals the kind of "somebody" we want to become (i.e., a language teacher) and autonomy signals our capacity to channel learning efforts in that direction'. He goes on to define teacher autonomy as situational, i.e. 'the freedom granted to teachers to exercise their discretion in teaching' and attributional, i.e. 'teachers' internal capacity to exercise the freedom productively' (Benson, 2016: 20). According to Benson, studies of teacher autonomy tend either to emphasise structural constraints on teachers or foreground their capacity to create spaces within these constraints. But Foucault (1977) himself saw power as a source of creativity and change, not only constraint. This is also illustrated by the teachers in this book who have all been willing to change and grow. Aurora relates how she never said 'no' to the company that she worked for – until she was in a position to set the agenda herself. Recently, language teaching courses have come under fire for their role in attempting to shape people to meet the demands of the neoliberal political economy (Block & Gray, 2016), while paying lip service to social justice (Morgan, 2016). These are valid concerns, but teacher education in the form of costly teaching certificates and training seminars, for example, plays an important part in the stories of the Filipino teachers. It is something they believe they must do as part of their professional development, and if there are obstacles to participation in existing organisations, then they create their own. In other words, they buy into the system, but they also create new structures, such as FETJ and the Jolly English school, that can help level the playing field for Filipinos. Nevertheless, English teaching in Japan is still not a level playing field: the local BoEs who employ Lori and Katrina are those that have a relationship with FETJ; not all BoEs in Japan view Filipino English teachers so favourably. Moreover, the institutional role of assistant language teachers (ALTs) remains problematic, despite efforts to define and encourage team-teaching in the Japanese classroom. Given this enduring situation of structural disparity, how should we evaluate the efforts of FETJ in the role of advocacy?

Returning to Benson's definition of identity, where does the desire to become 'somebody' come from in the first place? This is not a chicken-and-egg question. The answer for Taylor (1989, 1994) and Honneth (1995, 2012) is in the intersubjective recognition of the other as a 'somebody' or at least as someone with the potential to become a 'somebody'. This is the motivation behind Aurora's initiative to help fellow Filipinos who felt 'unable to speak up'. She recognises their potential to become language teachers. This motivation is even more apparent in the social activism that Lori engaged in with her partner, the social activist Cesar Santoyo. FETJ began life as an act of generosity by Aurora, inviting people round to her house to practice teaching methods they felt unable to try with other non-Filipino teachers. But it was its merger with Santoyo's Community and Home-based English Teachers (CHOBET) that transformed the group into a conscious collective mission to address discrimination, in other words, identity politics.

Identity politics is a loaded term (Bolinger, 1980) that comes with a great deal of historical and emotional baggage and, nowadays, with some harsh criticism (Murray, 2019). Kamhi-Stein (2016) goes to some lengths to explain why non-native English-speaking teachers (NNEST) in teaching English as a second language (TESOL) constitutes a 'movement', but does not go so far as to call it identity politics. She describes the achievements of the NNEST movement in creating opportunities for leadership development, and research and publications. However, she acknowledges that it has only been partially successful in providing NNEST professionals with networking opportunities and has failed overall to promote a more inclusive environment for such teachers. Similar objectives are espoused by FETJ: the group has created opportunities for leadership development, though not for research or publishing, apart from their self-published teacher guidelines handbook and teaching materials. It could thus be argued that FETJ is more successful in areas where the NNEST movement has been only partially or not at all successful. Participants who complete the FETJ teacher training seminars can use their certificates of completion to help them get work with the teacher dispatch companies, and the best participants are recommended for more prestigious and secure positions with the BoEs. For Filipinos, the group offers an inclusive and supportive environment, a sense of community and a sense of pride. This is the purpose of the national symbols that struck me so forcibly when I first started attending the FETJ events: the flag, the national anthem, the costumes, the folk dances and so on.

But these symbols of national pride are also what makes the group exclusive and this is the downside of identity politics. Aurora claims that the group is for anyone who wants to learn to teach, but clearly many of the group's practices are likely to appear exotic, if not alien and off-putting to many non-Filipinos. This is not to denigrate the work of FETJ, but to highlight the problem of identity politics, namely, that the promotion and celebration of an identity that has been marginalised or oppressed in the past does not necessarily lead to greater acceptance by others. As we saw in Renata's and Carmela's narratives, not only non-Filipinos, but even not all Filipinos necessarily feel welcome in this environment.

FETJ is a group that has been overtly involved in identity politics, since its avowed mission is to enhance the status of Filipinos and promote multiculturalism in Japan. Few other LTAs in Japan can claim to be engaged in social activism to this extent, although Women Educators and Language Learners (WELL), a volunteer organisation focusing on women's issues, is one that might qualify. Nevertheless, many language teachers join LTAs for a variety of reasons, some of which include opportunities for leadership and networking that are closed to them in other areas of their working lives (Paran, 2016; Stephenson, 2018; Stewart & Miyahara, 2016). Much of the research into language teacher identity focuses on teachers working in tertiary educational contexts, because that is where most researchers work. This is a very limited view of the language teaching field, one that omits the vast majority of language teachers. If language teacher identity is to be considered in sociopolitical or political economic terms, then a widening of the research horizon to areas where most teachers work is essential.

Identity Metaphors: Problematising Concepts

As I discussed in Chapter 3, Bourdieu's (1977, 1984, 1990) social theory has provided applied linguists with powerful concepts for understanding identity, particularly *habitus*, *field* and *capital*. Most notably, Bonny Norton expanded the economic metaphor of capital in her highly influential thesis that *investment*, the sociological equivalent of motivation, can explain how learners' efforts to change themselves in the process of mastering another language can be either propelled or hindered by social and ideological factors (Norton, 2001, 2013; Norton Peirce, 1995). More recently, Darvin and Norton's (2015) model places investment at the intersection of identity, capital and ideology. My argument in Chapter 3 is that the notion of investment risks being aligned with a neoliberal ideology in which the individual is construed as *homo economicus* (Block, 2018), motivated primarily by self-interest.

Nevertheless, although I wanted to argue against investment as a metaphor for identity, in its literal sense, as an expenditure of money or a foregoing of earnings in the present with the expectation of future income or profit, it is, in fact, pertinent in the stories of all the teachers. Thus, Lori was willing to forego proper payment for her first classes for kindergarteners as she saw that English teaching could be her 'bread and butter' in the future. Later, she mentions the large sums of money she paid to participate in teacher training seminars around Japan to gain knowledge she felt that she lacked. Investment in the form of teacher education courses, some of which cost a relatively large amount of money, is also evident in the younger teachers' stories: Anna Marie mentions that she took courses when she was pregnant and had a baby, since she was unable to start teaching at that time; Shin relates how he took a course with the University of Oregon; and Katrina explains how she took 18 extra credits as part of her bachelor's degree in order to gain a license to teach in the Philippines.

Elma is the only one of the nine narrators to use the term ('*that was my first investment with the money I was earning from teaching in Japan*'), but her usage refers not to any actions or intentions concerning her own identity as an English teacher but rather to actual investment using the savings from her work in Japan to found a pre-school in the Philippines and provide support for three of her siblings to move to Japan. Elsewhere in her narrative, Elma's pride in her identity as an English teacher hinges not on material success, but on recognition. The *eikaiwa* that employs her after the American school went bankrupt does not usually employ Filipinos, and therefore she has to excel as a teacher to prove herself. This is also what she tells younger Filipinos she meets ('*Once you show them that you are better than other teachers, they respect you and like you*').

As I have shown in the subsequent narratives, recognition is hugely important for most of these teachers. Sampaguita wins accolades from the very first school she goes to, without any formal teacher training or preparation. The younger teachers are recognised as stars by Aurora and are given positions of responsibility within the FETJ. Carmela expects to encounter some discrimination in Japan as a non-native speaker of English but, despite some setbacks in the beginning, is recognised for her expertise by the BoE and by her university employers. Among all the teachers here, Renata is the only one who is most ambivalent about an identity as an English teacher. She taught English in an *eikaiwa* because it was suggested to her by other Filipinos and because she felt she could do it well (although she says that anyone can teach), but the professional identity she aspires to has never been as an English teacher; rather, it has fluctuated between working in the media and having a career as an academic.

I cannot claim that financial metaphors have no part to play in identity. Neoliberal ideals have permeated our everyday thinking (Block, 2014, 2018; Block *et al.*, 2012; Chun, 2017); the language of capitalism has given us metaphors to live by (Lakoff & Johnson, 1980). The Filipino English teachers in this book were chosen because theirs are stories of success – successes that are recognised and vaunted by the groups to which they belong. But we can see the downside of living in a neoliberal world, particularly in the case of Lori's precarious start to teaching in public schools, or in the case of Elma's downward trajectory in Japan as her intersectional identities (Block & Corona, 2016) as an older Filipino woman impact on her 'value' to the *eikaiwa* market. Financial metaphors that extend the notion of monetary value into most areas of life do not seem out of place in today's world. I have to confess that they are part of my own thinking and my own linguistic repertoire too. Readers may have noticed that, in my own story in Chapter 1, I mention 'social capital' to invoke my own social status and social networks that have enabled me to build a career as an English teacher and academic in Japan from the mid-1990s onwards. I find Bourdieu's use of concepts such as social capital or symbolic capital to be extremely helpful for thinking about social stratification. My point is, however, that such theoretical uses of economic metaphors risk slipping into the neoliberal conceptualisation of identity in terms of monetary value, where a person's worth is determined by market forces rather than by principles of social justice. My goal in writing this critique is not so much to change the discourse of neo-liberalism as to call attention to the implications of using this discourse in our field and to suggest that there may be alternative ways to talk about and around teacher identity. The theories of identity as recognition that I have explored in this book (particularly Honneth, 1995, 2012) suggest that, rather than 'ideology' and 'capital', we could be looking more closely into ways in which individuals or groups are recognised or misrecognised, or how they achieve recognition, in civil society (cultural practices of politeness and respect) and in and through legal structures (institutions and policies).

Teacher Communities: Mutual Recognition

Although it is around the narratives of individual teachers that this book is organised, it is the organisation – FETJ – that brings them all together, including the two teachers who do not consider themselves to be members. In Chapter 4, I explored FETJ's identity as an LTA and came to the conclusion that it differs significantly from many other LTAs because one of its major goals is to enable members to enter the profession of teaching, whereas LTAs generally draw their membership from people who are already working as teachers. In particular, I wanted to show that FETJ's identity has been far from fixed or stable but has evolved over time due to the influence of personalities within the organisation and of changing circumstances in Japan. It has thus evolved from a small study group to a larger social activist enterprise to a still larger organisation offering training and support for aspiring English teachers. But although its functions have evolved over time, the national Filipino identity with which it originated has not changed, largely, it must be presumed, because of the name that the organisation bears and by which it is legally recognised. We have seen as well that FETJ was instrumental in launching the English teaching careers of three younger teachers, but it is clear that the teachers are also potential agents of change within FETJ, as Shin takes charge of a social event in Kanagawa and Anna Marie and Katrina move into positions of responsibility in FETJ and in the new Jolly English *eikaiwa* that it sets up.

Throughout the book, I have referred to FETJ as a *community*, but I have not clarified what is meant by this term. Community is a large and complex notion that has stimulated theory and research across a range of disciplines, including our own. It found particular purchase in the 1990s and 2000s, when I was writing my doctoral thesis (Stewart, 2005), through the proposal of theoretical models such as *community of practice* (Lave & Wenger, 1991; Wenger, 1998; Wenger *et al.*, 2002), *discourse communities* (Swales, 1990, 1998), *disciplinary communities* (Becher, 1989) and *professional discourse communities* (Tsui, 2003). A common characteristic of these concepts is the focus on the knowledge or domain and the specific practices that distinguish the group. I would argue now that a problem with this way of thinking about communities is that it places too much emphasis on discourse and not enough on the relationships that bind the group together.

The affective aspect of community was famously highlighted by the sociologist Zygmunt Bauman (2001) who declared that a community 'feels good', and that we all seek to be 'in a community' or 'have a community' in order to escape the dangers of an insecure world. In the social activist phase of FETJ, when it merged with CHOBET under the leadership of Lori and Cesar, the emphasis was exactly that – on enabling and empowering Filipino women (mostly) to become more secure in Japanese society. By sequencing the narratives according to the length of time spent in Japan, I have tried to show that the discrimination faced by Filipinos in the 1980s and 1990s, with its ensuing risks of poverty and violence, is far less prevalent in the late 2010s. Safety and security may still be one factor that motivates Filipinos to join FETJ, but I would argue that it misses the mark in explaining why the group is attractive and why some of its participants choose to stay involved after they have finished the training courses and found work as teachers.

Recently, the notion of community has been addressed again in an article proposing a new 'transdisciplinary' framework for understanding language acquisition that was published by a group of researchers under the name of The Douglas Fir Group (2015). Based on Urie Bronfenbrenner's (1979) bioecological model of development, the framework is helpful for conceptualising the thoroughgoing embeddedness and interconnectedness of individuals (including their neurological mechanisms and cognitive capacities) with the contexts, at various levels, in which they live. Although emotions do not figure in the graphic representation of the model, social interaction is explained by the Douglas Fir authors as inherently pleasurable and conducive to motivation. If this model is applied to FETJ, it could be argued that teachers join the group and continue to participate in its activities purely because they find pleasure and utility in it. But this does not explain their voluntary commitment to the group or the feelings of loyalty and gratitude that they express, which a recognition approach to identity does explain.

Honneth's theory of recognition differs significantly from an ecological model, in the first place because it is not based on a metaphor (as the Douglas Fir Group model and Bronfenbrenner's original model obviously are). Instead, as I have argued, recognition theory is based on an ontological assumption that the world consists of actual, identifiable social groups or spheres, in which recognition or misrecognition is revealed by real and powerfully felt emotions. Thus, in the domestic sphere, recognition is shown in the form of love; in the social sphere, it takes the form of respect; and in the legal sphere, it takes the form of rights. These three spheres are conceived of as separate by Honneth; however, judging from the teachers' narratives, there appears to be a significant overlap of the three, or even a struggle to change from one kind of sphere to another. We saw this in Sampaguita's story, for example, when she declares 'it can't be just a *mother–daughter relationship*, you have to have rules'. We can infer it too in Carmela's story in the relationship she had with the principal of the school where she first taught in the Philippines ('*she even called me her daughter-in-law!*'). The role of mentoring in teacher education generally has been a focus of research, including both its positive aspects (Curtis & de Yong, 2018; Delaney, 2012) and its dark side (Yuan, 2016). But a recognition approach could lead us to a closer focus on relationships: in official and unofficial mentorships, in ad hoc teaching communities (Stewart, 2007) and more institutionalised associations, and in wider society. This book is devoted to the position of Filipino English teachers in Japanese society exclusively through the stories of Filipino teachers. There is thus considerable scope for future research on how teachers are viewed by others – their students, parents, co-teachers and employers, in different teaching contexts – not only in formal educational institutions, but also in home-based teaching, *eikaiwa* businesses, community outreach classes provided by local governments and universities and so on.

Beyond Narratives

A great deal of the research on language teacher identity focuses on what Barkhuizen (2011) calls 'narrative knowledging', largely because narratives provide us with rich and detailed information on teachers' lives and work. As I discussed, narrative research covers an array of theoretical and methodological perspectives, but there is a broad consensus in current research that identities are discursive constructions and that they are constructed in interaction in specific situations (e.g. Barkhuizen, 2014; Bamberg *et al.*, 2011; Pavlenko, 2007). Narrative research – indeed qualitative research generally – calls for researcher reflexivity, whereby the researcher openly acknowledges and questions their role in the research process and the effect on the narrative that is told. I have chosen to do this by including my own story and by highlighting, at times, biases, blind spots or simply uncertainty in my interpretation of others' stories.

In the introduction to her book *Interrogating Privilege*, Stephanie Vandrick writes,

> I find myself writing in generalizations and in academicspeak. I need to do so in order to explain the book to readers, especially, first, on the topic of privilege and, second, on my reasons for the choice I have made to write very personally. So I am caught in a contradiction: I seem to need to write in a somewhat traditional academic style in this introduction before getting to the chapters that combine academic analysis with personal narratives. (Vandrick, 2009: 1)

This issue of style and voice is one that has preoccupied me too, first in collecting and transcribing the narratives, and now, in weaving my commentary and theorising – my 'academicspeak' – around those stories. As I have argued, the transcription and presentation of narratives involve numerous authorial choices, all of which are political in their implications.

It is customary to consider qualitative interviews as co-constructed meaning, or 'interViews', to cite the hugely influential Steinar Kvale (1996). However, in choosing to present the narratives in their entirety, my aim has been to convey the impression that these are *not* co-constructions. They may be considered *re*-constructions, in that they are remade for the printed page, an act that involves dealing with issues of incompatible speech/writing conventions, such as accent or punctuation. But I do not claim ownership of these stories: I have interpreted them, but they remain open to interpretations that may differ from the one I offer.

I could have chosen to write this book differently. In a book that claims to highlight identity politics, I could have – some readers may argue that I *should* have – asked the narrators for their interpretations – of their own narratives, and of my commentary about and around them. A considerable amount of research on language teacher identity involves teachers doing research on themselves as a form of reflexive practice (Barkhuizen, 2016c; Johnson & Golombek, 2002). Elsewhere, inclusive practitioner research (Allwright & Hanks, 2009; Hanks, 2017, 2019) has been gaining ground as a principled approach to conducting research with, rather than on other people. Both of these approaches have much to recommend them and I, for one, look forward to reading new research by, or in collaboration with Filipino teachers working across the range of educational contexts.

Epilogue

In April 2017, I was granted a year's sabbatical from the university I work for in Japan. One of my primary aims during the year was to write this book. Since I had never visited the Philippines, despite my interest and involvement with FETJ, I arranged to spend the first month of the sabbatical there. My plan was to tour around the islands of Palawan and Luzon to get a sense of where the teachers whose stories I had collected were coming from. I received help and advice from the teachers in this book: Sampaguita helped me by agreeing to give me a crash course in Tagalog before I went. Carmela helped me by finding a tour agent who organised transport and accommodation for my two island road trips. Elma helped me by introducing me to her sister Ethel, who showed me round the Montessori pre-school they founded in honour of their mother, and who found me a driver to ferry me round Manila in my last two days in the country.

My contacts in the Philippines were not limited to those I obtained through FETJ. I also spent an evening and a day with a family I had known indirectly for many years. Julie was my cleaning lady and babysitter in Japan. Her main job was as a cleaner for an embassy, one of the few exceptions to Japan's denial of visas for domestic work, but outside of the embassy job, Julie had other jobs working as a cleaner for people like me. Although they always seemed to be working, Julie and her husband Luisito always managed to find time to help us out. They helped us move house, and Julie helped us find furniture for the new place. In return, I helped Julie by writing testimonials and letters, enabling her to travel to the United States to visit relatives, and to pursue an insurance claim when her oldest son crashed their car. We talked about our children mostly. I listened to her worries about her three children, growing up in the Philippines, their care and education all paid for by Julie's cleaning work and Luisito's factory and packing jobs in Japan.

I met up with two of those children in Manila. Rizza Joy was born in Manila before Julie moved to Japan and now works as a nurse in a military hospital. JL was born 15 years later and is now a college student studying management in the hospitality industry. They arrived at my guesthouse and took me off to dinner, Rizza Joy's husband Paul driving their Toyota jeep, and Rizza Joy, JL, JL's girlfriend, Patty, and Rizza Joy's and Paul's three young children, aged eight, four and three, all crammed into the back seat. The next day, a Saturday, the eight of us piled back into the jeep and inched south along congested roads to a resort hotel on a high escarpment from which we could view the Taal Volcano, its tiny hillock and crater dwarfed by the massive caldera lake which surrounds it. We talked about our lives and our plans for the future. Paul, whose mother had lived and worked as an entertainer in Japan all his life, had met Rizza Joy when both of them were training to be nurses. Julie had wanted them to move to Japan to work under a special scheme that was intended to admit nurses and caregivers from Asian countries, such as the Philippines. But Rizza Joy and Paul were keener to try English-speaking countries and had their sights set on Australia. Paul was retraining as a pastry chef, an occupation for which Australia was currently permitting immigrants, and was supplementing the family income in Manila by teaching English via Skype for an English language teaching company. JL and Patty were both first-year university students but they also already had ambitions to work abroad. Patty was studying to be an English teacher and told me that her parents were very keen for her to go overseas to work. She told me how much she would be likely to earn as a public school teacher in the Philippines: less than a quarter of what she could make as a dispatch company English teacher in Japan. I told her about my connection to Filipino English Teacher of Japan and promised to send her their contact details.

References

Abrams, D. and Hogg, M.A. (eds) (1990) *Social Identity Theory: Constructive and Critical Advances*. London: Harvester-Wheatsheaf.

Agudo, J.D.M. (ed.) (2018) *Emotions in Second Language Teaching*. Basel: Springer.

Ahmed, S. (2004) *The Cultural Politics of Emotion*. Edinburgh: Edinburgh University Press.

Allwright, D. and Hanks, J. (2009) *The Developing Language Learner: An Introduction to Exploratory Practice*. Basingstoke: Palgrave Macmillan.

Althusser, L. (1971) Ideology and ideological state apparatuses (Notes towards an investigation). *Lenin and Philosophy and Other Essays* (B. Brewster, trans.). London: Verso.

Andrews, M., Squire, C. and Tamboukou, M. (2013) *Doing Narrative Research*. London: Sage.

Antaki, C. and Widdicombe, S. (1998) *Identities in Talk*. London: Sage.

Appleby, R. (2016) Researching privilege in language teacher identity. *TESOL Quarterly* 50 (3), 755–768.

Asher, J. (1996) *Learning Another Language Through Actions* (5th edn). Los Gatos, CA: Sky Oaks Productions.

Atkinson, R. (1998) *The Life Story Interview*. Thousand Oaks, CA: Sage.

Aubrey, J. and Coombe, C. (2010) The TESOL Arabia conference and its role in the professional development of teachers at institutions of higher education in the United Arab Emirates. *Academic Leadership Journal* 8 (3). See https://scholars.fhsu.edu/cgi/viewcontent.cgi?article=1496&context=alj. Accessed Dec 1, 2019.

Austin, J.L. (1976) *How to Do Things With Words* (2nd edn). Oxford: Oxford University Press.

Bamberg, M. (2007) *Narrative: State of the Art*. Amsterdam: John Benjamins.

Bamberg, M., de Fina, A., and Schiffrin, D. (2011) Discourse and identity construction. In S. Schwartz, K. Luyckx and V. Vignoles (eds) *Handbook of Identity Theory and Research* (pp. 177–199). New York: Springer.

Bamberg, M. and McCabe, A. (2000) *Narrative Identity*. Amsterdam: John Benjamins.

Barkhuizen, G. (2008) A narrative approach to exploring context in language teaching. *English Language Teaching Journal* 62 (3), 231–239.

Barkhuizen, G. (2011) Narrative knowledging in TESOL. *TESOL Quarterly* 45 (3), 391–414.

Barkhuizen, G. (ed.) (2014) *Narrative Research in Applied Linguistics*. Cambridge: Cambridge University Press.

Barkhuizen, G. (2016a) Language teacher identity research: An introduction. In G. Barkhuizen (ed.) *Reflections on Language Teacher Identity Research* (pp. 1–11). New York: Routledge.

Barkhuizen, G. (ed.) (2016b) *Reflections on Language Teacher Identity Research*. New York: Routledge.

Barkhuizen, G. (2016c) Narrative approaches to exploring language, identity and power in language teacher education. *RELC Journal* 47 (1), 25–42.

Barkhuizen, G., Benson, P. and Chik, A. (2014) *Narrative Inquiry in Language Teaching and Learning Research*. New York: Routledge.

Bauman, Z. (2001) *Community: Seeking Safety in an Insecure World*. Cambridge: Polity.

Baynham, M. (2011) Stance, positioning, and alignment in narratives of professional experiences. *Language in Society* 40 (1), 63–74.

Becher, T. (1989) *Academic Tribes and Territories*. Buckingham: SRHE and Open University Press.

Becker, G.S. (1964) *Human Capital: A Theoretical and Empirical Analysis, with Special Reference to Education* (3rd edn). Chicago, IL: University of Chicago Press.

Benesch, S. (2012) *Considering Emotions in Critical English Language Teaching: Theories and Praxis*. New York: Routledge.

Benesch, S. (2017) *Emotions and English Language Teaching: Considering Teachers' Emotion Labour*. New York: Routledge.

Benson, P. (2016) Teacher autonomy and teacher agency. In G. Barkhuizen (ed.) *Reflections on Language Teacher Identity Research* (pp. 18–23). New York: Routledge.

Bhaskar, R. (1998) *The Possibility of Naturalism* (3rd edn). London: Routledge.

Bhaskar, R. (2002) *From Science to Emancipation: Alienation and the Actuality of Enlightenment*. London: Sage.

Block, D. (2007) *Second Language Identities*. London: Continuum.

Block, D. (2013) The structure and agency dilemma in identity and intercultural communication research. *Language and Intercultural Communication* 13 (2), 126–147.

Block, D. (2014) *Social Class in Applied Linguistics*. London: Routledge.

Block, D. (2018) *Political Economy and Sociolinguistics*. London: Bloomsbury.

Block, D. and Corona, V. (2016) Intersectionality in language and identity research. In S. Preece (ed.) *The Routledge Handbook of Language and Identity* (pp. 507–522). London: Routledge.

Block, D. and Gray, J. (2016) 'Just go away and do it and you get marks': The degradation of language teaching in neoliberal times. *Journal of Multilingual and Multicultural Development* 37 (5), 481–494.

Block, D., Gray, J. and Holborow, M. (2012) *Neoliberalism and Applied Linguistics*. London: Routledge.

Blommaert, J. (2005) *Discourse: A Critical Introduction*. Cambridge: Cambridge University Press.

Blommaert, J. (2015) Pierre Bourdieu: Perspectives on language in society. In J.O. Ostman and J. Vershueren (eds) *Handbook of Pragmatics* (pp. 1–16). Amsterdam: John Benjamins.

Bolinger, D. (1980) *Language: The Loaded Weapon*. London: Taylor & Francis.

Boltanski, L. and Chiapello, E. (2017) *The New Spirit of Capitalism* (G. Elliott, trans.). London: Verso.

Bourdieu, P. (1977) *Outline of a Theory of Practice* (R. Nice, trans.). Cambridge: Cambridge University Press.

Bourdieu, P. (1984) *Distinction: A Social Critique of the Judgement of Taste* (R. Nice, trans.). Cambridge, MA: Harvard University Press.

Bourdieu, P. (1990) *The Logic of Practice* (R. Nice, trans.). Cambridge: Polity.

Bourdieu, P. (1991) *Language and Symbolic Power* (G. Raymond and M. Adamson, trans.). Cambridge, MA: Harvard University Press.

Brewer, M. and Gardner, W. (1996) Who is this 'we'? Levels of collective identity and self-representation. *Journal of Personality and Social Psychology* 71, 83–93.

Bronfenbrenner, U. (1979) *The Ecology of Human Development*. Cambridge, MA: Harvard University Press.

Bruner, J. (1986) *Actual Minds, Possible Worlds*. Cambridge, MA: Harvard University Press.

Bruner, J. (1990) *Acts of Meaning*. Cambridge, MA: Harvard University Press.

Bucholtz, M. (2000) The politics of transcription. *Journal of Pragmatics* 32, 1439–1465.

Butler, Y. and Iino, M. (2005) Current Japanese reforms in English language education: The 2003 'action plan'. *Language Policy* 4 (1), 25–45.

Cameron, D., Frazer, E., Harvey, P., Rampton, M.B.H. and Richardson, K. (1992) *Researching Language: Issues of Power and Method*. London: Routledge.

Carless, D. (2006) Good practices in team teaching in Japan, South Korea and Hong Kong. *System* 34 (3), 341–351.

Cheung, E. (2005) Hong Kong secondary schoolteachers' understanding of their careers. *Teachers and Teaching* 11 (2), 127–149.

Cheung, Y.L., Said, S.B. and Park, K. (2015) *Advances and Current Trends in Language Teacher Identity Research*. New York: Routledge.

Chun, C.W. (2017) *The Discourses of Capitalism: Everyday Economists and the Production of Common Sense*. London: Routledge.

Cook, V. (1992) Evidence for multicompetence. *Language Learning* 42 (4), 557–591.

Cook, V. (2008) *Second Language Learning and Language Teaching*. London: Arnold.

Crenshaw, K. (1989) Demarginalizing the intersection of race and sex: A black feminist critique of antidiscrimination doctrine, feminist theory and antiracist politics. *University of Chicago Legal Forum* 1989 (1), 139–167. See https://chicagounbound.uchicago.edu/uclf/vol1989/iss1/8. Accessed Dec 1, 2019.

Crenshaw, K. (1991) Mapping the margins: Intersectionality, identity politics and violence against women of colour. *Stanford Law Review* 43 (6), 1241–1299.

Currie-Robson, C. (2015) *English to Go: Inside Japan's Teaching Sweatshops*. Amazon Createspace.

Curtis, A. and de Yong, E. (2018) Formalizing language teacher association leadership development. In A. Elsheikh, C. Coombe and O. Effiong. (2018). *The Role of Language Teacher Associations in Professional Development* (pp. 241–253). Basel: Springer.

Darvin, R. and Norton, B. (2015) Identity and a model of investment in applied linguistics. *Annual Review of Applied Linguistics* 35, 36–56.

De Costa, P. (ed.) (2015) *Ethics in Applied Linguistics Research: Language Researcher Narratives*. New York: Routledge.

De Costa, P. and Norton, B. (eds) (2017) Introduction: Identity, transdisciplinarity, and the good language teacher. *The Modern Language Journal* [Supplement: Transdisciplinarity and Language Teacher Identity] 101 (S1), 3–14.

De Fina, A. (2011) Discourse and identity. In T.A. Van Dijk (ed.) *Discourse Studies: A Multidisciplinary Introduction* (pp. 263–282). Thousand Oaks, CA: Sage.

De Fina, A. (2016) Linguistic practices and transnational identities. In S. Preece (ed.) *The Routledge Handbook of Language and Identity* (pp. 163–178). London: Routledge.

De Fina, A. and Perrino, S. (2013) Transnational identities. *Applied Linguistics* 34 (5), 509–515

Delaney, Y. (2012) Research on mentoring language teachers: Its role in language education. *Foreign Language Annals* 45 (S1), 184–202.

Dickey, R. (2018) Representativeness and development of leaders in Korea TESOL. In A. Elsheikh, C. Coombe and O. Effiong (eds) *The Role of Language Teacher Associations in Professional Development* (pp. 267–282). Basel: Springer.

Docot, L. (2009) On identity and development: Filipino women entertainers in transition in Japan. In D. Nault (ed.) *Development in Asia: Interdisciplinary, Post-Neoliberal, and Transnational Perspectives* (pp. 107–134). Boca Raton, FL: Brown Walker Press.

Duchêne, A. and Heller, M. (2012) *Language in Late Capitalism: Pride and Profit*. London: Routledge.

Duff, P. (2015) Transnationalism, multilingualism, and identity. *Annual Review of Applied Linguistics* 35, 57–80.

Early, M. and Norton, B. (2014) Revisiting English as medium of instruction in rural African classrooms. *Journal of Multilingual and Multicultural Development* 35 (7), 1–18.

Edwards, D. (1998) The relevant thing about her: Social identity categories in use. In C. Antaki and S. Widdicombe (eds) *Identities in Talk* (pp. 15–33). Thousand Oaks, CA: Sage.

Ehlers-Savala, F. (2012) Advocacy in language teaching. *The Encyclopaedia of Applied Linguistics*. See https://onlinelibrary.wiley.com/doi/10.1002/9781405198431.wbeal0010. Accessed Dec 1, 2019.

Elsheikh, A., Coombe, C. and Effiong, O. (2018) *The Role of Language Teacher Associations in Professional Development*. Basel: Springer.

Fabiani, J.-L. (2016) *Pierre Bourdieu: Un Structuralisme Héroïque*. Paris: Seuil.

Foucault, M. (1977) *Discipline and Punish: The Birth of the Prison* (A. Sheridan, trans.). New York: Random House.

Foucault, M. (1980) *Power/Knowledge: Selected Interviews and Writings 1972–77* (C. Gordon, ed.; C. Gordon, L. Marshall, J. Mepham and K. Soper, trans.). New York: Pantheon.

Foucault, M. (1988) *Technologies of the Self: A Seminar with Michel Foucault*. Boston, MA: University of Massachusetts Press.

Fraser, N. (2000) Rethinking recognition. *New Left Review* 3, 107–120.

Fraser, N. (2009) *Scales of Justice: Reimagining Political Space in a Globalizing World*. New York: Columbia University Press.

Fraser, N. (2013) *Fortunes of Feminism: From State-Managed Capitalism to Neoliberal Crisis*. London: Verso.

Fraser, N. and Honneth, A. (2003) *Redistribution or Recognition: A Political-Philosophical Exchange*. London: Verso.

Garton, S. and Richards, K. (eds) (2008) *Professional Encounters in TESOL: Discourses of Teachers in Teaching*. Basingstoke: Palgrave.

Gee, J.P., Hull, G. and Lankshear, C. (1996) *The New Work Order: Behind the Language of New Capitalism*. Boulder, CO: Westview Press.

Georgakopolou, A. (2007) *Small Stories, Interaction and Identities*. Amsterdam: John Benjamins.

Georgakopolou, A. (2015) Small stories research. In A. De Fina and A. Georgakopolou, (eds) *The Handbook of Narrative Analysis* (pp. 255–272). Oxford: Wiley.

Giddens, A. (1991) *Modernity and Self-Identity: Self and Society in the Late Modern Age*. Stanford, CA: Stanford University Press.

Gordon. J.A., Fujita. H., Kariya. T. and LeTendre. G. (eds) (2010) *Challenges to Japanese Education*. New York: Teachers College Press.

Gray, J. and Morton, T. (2018) *Social Interaction and English Language Teacher Identity*. Edinburgh: Edinburgh University Press.

Green, D. (2017) As its population ages Japan quietly turns to immigration. *Migration Policy Institute*. See https://www.migrationpolicy.org/article/its-population-ages-japan-quietly-turns-immigration. Accessed Dec 1, 2019

Grint, K. (2005) *The Sociology of Work* (3rd edn). Cambridge: Polity.

Handy, C. (2015) *The Second Curve: Thoughts on Reinventing Society*. London: Random House.

Hanks, J. (2017) *Exploratory Practice in Language Teaching: Puzzling about Principles and Practices*. Basingstoke: Palgrave.

Hanks, J. (2019) From research-as-practice to exploratory practice-as-research in language teaching and beyond. *Language Teaching* 52 (2), 143–187.

Harrison, J. and Prado, J. (2019) Problematizing advocacy: Definitions, alignments and contradictions. In H. Linville and J. Whiting (eds) *Advocacy in ELT and English Language Learning* (Chapter 2). New York: Routledge.

Hashimoto, K. (2013) The construction of the 'native-speaker' in Japan's educational policies for TEFL. In S. Houghton and D. Rivers (eds) *Native-Speakerism in Japan:*

Intergroup Dynamics in Foreign Language Education (pp. 159–168). Bristol: Multilingual Matters.

Hayes, D. (2005) Exploring the lives of non-native speaking English educators in Sri Lanka. *Teachers and Teaching: Theory and Practice* 11 (2), 169–194.

Hayes, D. (2010) Duty and service: Life and career of a Tamil teacher of English in Sri Lanka. *TESOL Quarterly* 44 (1), 58–83.

Hayes, B. (2013) Hiring criteria for Japanese university English teaching faculty. In S. Houghton and D. Rivers (eds) *Native-Speakerism in Japan: Intergroup Dynamics in Foreign Language Education* (pp. 132–146). Bristol: Multilingual Matters.

Held, J., McGrew, A., Goldblatt, D. and Perraton, J. (1999) *Global Transformations: Economics, Politics and Culture*. Cambridge: Polity.

Heller, M. and Duchêne, A. (2012) Pride and profit: Changing discourses of language, capital and nation-state. In A. Duchêne and M. Heller (eds) *Language in Late Capitalism: Pride and Profit* (pp. 1–21). London: Routledge.

Hermans, H. (2002) The person as a motivated storyteller: Valuation theory and the self-confrontation method. In R. Neimeyer and G. Neimeyer (eds) *Advances in Personal Construct Theory* (pp. 3–38). Westport, CT: Praeger.

Hester, S. and Eglin, P. (1997) Membership categorization analysis: An introduction. In S. Hester and P. Eglin (eds) *Culture in Action: Studies in Membership Categorization-Analysis* (pp. 1–23). Washington, DC: University Press of America.

Hochsschild, A.R. (1979) Emotion work, feeling rules, and social structure. *The American Journal of Sociology* 85 (3), 551–575.

Hogg, M.A. and Reid, S.A. (2006) Social identity, self-categorisation, and the communication of group norms. *Communication Theory* 16, 7–30.

Holliday, A. (2005) *The Struggle to Teach English as an International Language*. Oxford: Oxford University Press.

Holliday, A. (2006) Native-speakerism. *ELT Journal* 60 (4), 385–387.

Holliday, A. (2018) Native-Speakerism. *The TESOL Encyclopedia of English Language Teaching*. See https://onlinelibrary.wiley.com/doi/10.1002/9781118784235.eelt0027. Accessed Dec 1, 2019.

Honneth, A. (1995) *The Struggle for Recognition: The Moral Grammar of Social Conflicts*. Cambridge: Polity.

Honneth, A. (2012) *The I in We: Studies in the Theory of Recognition*. Cambridge: Polity.

Houghton, S. and Rivers, D. (2013) *Native-Speakerism in Japan: Intergroup Dynamics in Foreign Language Education*. Bristol: Multilingual Matters.

Houghton, S., Rivers, D. and Hashimoto, K. (2018) *Beyond Native-Speakerism: Current Explorations and Future Visions*. London: Routledge.

Huberman, M. (1993) *The Lives of Teachers* (J. Neufeld, trans.). New York: Teachers College Press.

Inokuchi, H. and Nozaki, Y. (2005) 'Different than us': Othering, orientalist and US middle school students' discourses on Japan. *Asia Pacific Journal of Education* 25, 61–74.

Irvine, J. and Gal, S. (2000) Language ideology and linguistic differentiation. In P.V. Kroskrity (ed.) *Regimes of Language: Ideologies, Polities and Identities* (pp. 35–83). Santa Fe, NM: School of American Research Press.

Jacques, M. (2016) The death of neoliberalism and the crisis in western politics. *The Guardian*, 21 August.

Jenkins, R. (1982) Bourdieu and the reproduction of determinism. *Sociology* 16 (2), 270–281.

JET Programme (n.d.) History. See http://jetprogramme.org/en/history/. Accessed Nov 29, 2019.

Johnson, K. and Golombek, P. (2002) *Teachers' Narrative Inquiry as Professional Development*. Cambridge: Cambridge University Press.

Johnston, B. (1997) Do EFL teachers have careers? *TESOL Quarterly* 31, 681–712.

Johnston, B. (1999) The expatriate teacher as postmodern paladin. *Research in the Teaching of English* 34, 255–280.

Johnston, B. (2003) *Values in English Language Teaching*. Mahwah, NJ: Lawrence Erlbaum.

Kachru, B. (1985) Standards, codification and sociolinguistic realism: The English language in the outer circle. In R. Quirk and H. Widdowson (eds) *English in the World* (pp. 11–30). Cambridge: Cambridge University Press.

Kalaja, P., Menezes, A. and Barcelos, M. (2008) *Narratives of Learning and Teaching EFL*. Basingstoke: Palgrave Macmillan.

Kamada, L. (2009) *Hybrid Identities and Adolescent Girls: Being Half in Japan*. Bristol: Multilingual Matters.

Kamhi-Stein, L.D. (2016) The nonnative English speaker teachers in TESOL movement. *ELT Journal* 70 (2), 180–189.

Kanno, Y. (2008) *Language and Education in Japan: Unequal Access to Bilingualism*. Basingstoke: Palgrave.

Kiernan, P. (2010) *Narrative Identity in English Language Teaching: Exploring Teacher Interviews in Japanese and English*. Basingstoke: Palgrave.

Kloss, L. (1999) The suitability and application of scenario planning for national professional associations. *Nonprofit Management and Leadership* 10, 71–83.

Koike, I. (2013) (ed.) *Proposals for English Education in Japan (Teigen: Nihon no Eigo Kyouiku)*. Tokyo: Mitsumura Tosho.

Kramsch, C. (2013) Afterword. In B. Norton *Identity and Language Learning: Extending the Conversation* (pp. 192–199; 2nd edn) Bristol: Multilingual Matters.

Kramsch, C. and Zhang, L. (2018) *The Multilingual Instructor*. Oxford: Oxford University Press.

Kubota, R. (1999) Japanese culture constructed by discourses: Implications for applied linguistic research and English language teaching. *TESOL Quarterly* 33 (1), 9–35.

Kubota, R. (2002) Impact of globalization on language teaching in Japan. In D. Block and D. Cameron (eds) *Globalization and Language Teaching* (pp. 13–28). London: Routledge.

Kubota, R. and Lin, A. (2009) *Race, Culture, and Identities in Second Language Education: Exploring Critically Engaged Practice*. New York: Routledge.

Kubota, R. and Fujimoto, D. (2013) Racialized native speakers: Voices of Japanese American English language professionals. In S. Houghton and D. Rivers (eds) *Native-Speakerism in Japan: Intergroup Dynamics in Foreign Language Education* (pp. 196–206). Bristol: Multilingual Matters.

Kumaravadivelu, B. (2014) The decolonial option in English language teaching: Can the subaltern act? *TESOL Quarterly* 50 (1), 66–85.

Kvale, S. (1996) *InterViews: An Introduction to Qualitative Research Interviewing*. London: Sage.

Labov, W. and Waletzky, J. (1967) Narrative analysis: Oral versions of personal experience. *Journal of Narrative and Life History* 7 (4), 3–38.

Lakoff, G. and Johnson, M. (1980) *Metaphors We Live By*. Urbana, IL: University of Chicago Press.

Lamb, T. (2012) Language associations and collaborative support: Language teacher associations as empowering spaces for professional networks. *Innovation in Language Learning and Teaching* 6, 287–308.

Lave, J. and Wenger, E. (1991) *Situated Learning: Legitimate Peripheral Participation*. Cambridge: Cambridge University Press.

Lie, J. (2001) *Multiethnic Japan*. Cambridge, MA: Harvard University Press.

Lin, A., Grant, R., Kubota, R., Motha, S., Tinker-Sachs, G. and Vandrick, S. (2004) Women faculty of colour in TESOL: Theorizing our experiences. *TESOL Quarterly* 38, 487–504.

Linville, H. and Whiting, J. (eds) (2019) *Advocacy in ELT and English Language Learning.* New York: Routledge.

Lippi-Green, R. (1997) *English with an Accent: Language, Ideology, and Discrimination in the United States.* New York: Routledge.

Liu, Y. and Xu, Y. (2011) Inclusion or exclusion?: A narrative inquiry of a language teacher's identity experience in the 'new work order' of competing pedagogies. *Teaching and Teacher Education* 27 (3), 589–597.

Lorente, B. (2012) The making of 'workers of the world': Language and the labour brokerage state. In A. Duchêne and M. Heller (eds) *Language in Late Capitalism: Pride and Profit* (pp. 183–206) New York: Routledge.

Lorente, B. (2017) *Scripts of Servitude: Language, Labour, and Transnational Domestic Work.* Bristol: Multilingual Matters.

Lortie, D. (1975) *Schoolteacher: A Sociological Study.* Urbana, IL: University of Chicago Press.

Luxton, M., Fennelly, R. and Fukuda, S. (2014) A survey of ALTs and JTEs. *Bulletin of Shikoku University* A42, 45–54.

MacIntyre, A. (1981) *After Virtue.* London: Bloomsbury.

MacPherson, S., Kouritzin, S. and Kim, S. (2005) Profits or professionalism: Issues facing the professionalization of TESL in Canada. *College Quarterly* 8 (2). See http://collegequarterly.ca/2005-vol08-num02-spring/macpherson_kouritzin_kim.html. Accessed Dec 1, 2019.

Maher, J. and Yashiro, K. (eds) (1995) *Multilingual Japan.* Bristol: Multilingual Matters.

Mandel, E. (1978) *Late Capitalism.* London: Verso.

Markus, H.R. and Kitayama, S. (1991) Culture and the self: Implications for cognition, emotion, and motivation. *Psychological Review* 98 (2), 224–253.

McConnell, D. (2000) *Importing Diversity: Inside Japan's JET Programme.* Berkley, CA: University of California Press.

McCrostie, J. (2017) As Japan's JET programme hits its 30s, the jury's still out. *The Japan Times.* See https://www.japantimes.co.jp/community/2017/05/03/issues/japans-jet-programme-hits-30s-jurys-still/#.XJSC5dHgpPM. Accessed Dec 1, 2019.

McNay, L. (2008) *Against Recognition.* Cambridge: Polity.

McQueen, P. (2015) *Subjectivity, Gender, and The Struggle for Recognition.* Basingstoke: Palgrave Macmillan.

Menard-Warwick, J. (2014) *English Language Teachers on the Discursive Faultlines: Identities, Ideologies and Pedagogies.* Bristol: Multilingual Matters.

Metzgar, E. (2017) *The JET Programme and the U.S.-Japan Relationship: A Goodwill Goldmine.* Laynham, MA: Lexington Books.

Ministry of Education, Culture, Sports, Science and Technology (n.d.) *English Education Reform Plan Corresponding to Globalization.* See http://www.mext.go.jp/en/news/topics/detail/__icsFiles/afieldfile/2014/01/23/1343591_1.pdf.

Ministry of Health, Labour and Welfare (n.d.) *Handbook of Health and Welfare Statistics 2017.* See https://www.mhlw.go.jp/english/database/db-hh/1-2.html.

Ministry of Justice (2017). *Statistics on the Foreigners Registered in Japan,* see www.ipss.go.jp › p-info › e › psj2017 › PSJ2017-10.

Mischler, E. (1986) *Research Interviewing: Context and Narrative.* Cambridge, MA: Harvard University Press.

Miyahara, M. (2015) *Emerging Social Identities and Emotion in Foreign Language Learning: A Narrative-Oriented Approach.* Bristol: Multilingual Matters.

Morgan, B. (2004) Teacher identity as pedagogy: Toward a field-internal conceptualisation in bilingual and second language education. *International Journal of Bilingual Education and Bilingualism* 7 (2), 172–188.

Morgan, B. (2016) Language teacher identity and the domestication of dissent: An exploratory account. *TESOL Quarterly* 50 (3), 708–734.

Morgan, B. and Clarke, M. (2011) Identity in second language teaching and learning. In E. Hinkel (ed.) *Handbook of Research in Second Language Teaching and Learning* (pp. 817–836; Vol. 2). New York: Routledge.

Motha, S. (2014) *Race, Empire, and English Language Teaching: Creating Responsible and Ethical Anti-Racist Practice.* New York: Teacher College Press.

Motha, S. and Lin, A. (2014) Non-coercive rearrangements: Theorizing desire in TESOL. *TESOL Quarterly* 48 (2), 331–359.

Murai, S. (2016) Japan sees record number of high foreign residents. *The Japan Times.* See https://www.japantimes.co.jp/news/2016/03/11/national/japan-sees-record-high-number-foreign-residents-justice-ministry/#.XJSFLtHgpPM. Accessed Dec 1, 2019.

Murray, D. (2019) *The Madness of Crowds: Gender, Race and Identity.* London: Bloomsbury Continuum.

Nagatomo, D. (2012) *Exploring Japanese University Teachers Professional Identity.* Bristol: Multilingual Matters.

Nagatomo, D. (2013) The advantages and disadvantages faced by housewife English teachers in the cottage industry Eikaiwa business. *The Language Teacher* 37 (1), 3–7.

Nagatomo, D. (2016) *Identity, Gender, and Teaching English in Japan.* Bristol: Multilingual Matters.

Nilan, P. (1995) Membership categorisation devices under construction: Social identity boundary maintenance in everyday discourse. *Australian Review of Applied Linguistics* 18 (1), 69–94.

Noddings, N. (1984) *Caring: A Feminine Approach to Ethics and Moral Education.* Berkeley, CA: University of California Press.

Norton, B. (2000) *Identity and Language Learning: Gender, Ethnicity and Educational Change.* New York: Longman.

Norton, B. (2013) *Identity and Language Learning: Extending the Conversation* (2nd edn). Bristol: Multilingual Matters.

Norton, B. (2016) Learner investment and language teacher identity. In G. Barkhuizen (ed.) *Reflections on Language Teacher Identity* (pp. 80–87). New York: Routledge.

Norton Peirce, B. (1995) Social identity, investment and language learning. *TESOL Quarterly* 29 (1), 9–31.

Ochs, E. and Capps, L. (2001) *Living Narrative.* Cambridge, MA: Harvard University Press.

Ohno, S. (2007) Regaining Japaneseness: The politics of recognition by the Philippine nikkeijin. *Asian Studies Review* 31, 243–260.

Ohno, S. (2008) Transnational citizenship and deterritorialized identity: The meanings of Nikkei diasporas' shuttling between the Philippines and Japan. *Journal of Critical Perspectives on Asia* 44 (1), 1–22.

Ohno, S. and Iijima M. (2010) *Citizenships, Lives and Identities of the Philippine Nikkeijin Residing in Japan: Reports on the Results of a Nationwide Questionnaire Survey.* Fukuoka: Kyushu University. Kyushu University Asia Center.

Oishi, N. (2005) *Women in Motion. Globalization, State Policies, and Labor Migration in Asia.* Stanford, CA: Stanford University Press.

Osawa, M. and Kingston, J. (2010) *Risk and Consequences: The Changing Japanese Employment Paradigm.* New York: New York University Press.

Osumi, M. (2019) Number of foreign residents in Japan grew 6.6% in 2018, while number of overstayers grew almost twice as much, government data shows. *The Japan Times.* See https://www.japantimes.co.jp/news/2019/03/22/national/number-foreign-residents-japan-rose-6-6-2018-number-overstayers-grew-almost-twice-much-government-data-shows/#.XVk5nVB7mYU. Accessed Dec 1, 2019.

Ota, H. and Horiuchi, K. (2018) Internationalization through English medium instruction in Japan: Challenging a contemporary Dejima. In D. Proctor and L. Rumley (eds) *The Future Agenda of Internationalization in Higher Education* (pp. 15–27). New York: Routledge.

Otake, T. (2004) Insatiable thirst for English boosts language schools. *The Japan Times.* See https://www.japantimes.co.jp/news/2004/06/04/national/insatiable-thirst-for-english-boosts-language-schools/#.XJSEvdHgpPN. Accessed Dec 1, 2019.

Paran, A. (2016) Language teacher associations: Key themes and future directions. *ELT Journal* 70 (2), 127–136.

Parrenas, R. (2008) *The Force of Domesticity: Filipina Migrants and Globalisation.* New York: New York University Press.

Park, G. (2006) *Unsilencing the Silenced: The Journeys of Five East Asian Women with Implications for TESOL Teacher Education Programs.* College, MD: University of Maryland Press.

Park, G. (2017) *Narratives of East Asian Women Teachers of English: Where Privilege Meets Marginalization.* Bristol: Multilingual Matters.

Pavlenko, A. (2003) 'I never knew I was bilingual': Reimagining teacher identities in TESOL. *Journal of Language, Identity and Education* 2 (4), 251–268.

Pavlenko, A. (2007) Autobiographic narratives as data in applied linguistics. *Applied Linguistics* 28 (2), 163–188.

Phan, L.H. (2008) *Teaching English as an International Language: Identity, Resistance and Negotiation.* Clevedon: Multilingual Matters.

Phillipson, R. (1992) *Linguistic Imperialism.* Oxford: Oxford University Press.

Phoenix, A. (2013) Analysing narrative contexts. In M. Andrews, C. Squire and M. Tamboukou (eds) *Doing Narrative Research* (pp. 72–87; 2nd edn). London: Sage.

Piller, I. (2012) The sociolinguistics of nail care. *Language on the Move.* See https://www.languageonthemove.com/the-sociolinguistics-of-nail-care/. Accessed Dec 1, 2019.

Piller, I. and Takahashi, K. (2006) A passion for English: Desire and the language market. In A. Pavlenko (ed.) *Bilingual Minds: Emotional Experience, Expression, and Representation* (pp. 59–83). Clevedon: Multilingual Matters.

Polkinghorne, D. (1988) *Narrative Knowing and the Human Sciences.* Albany, NY: State University of New York Press.

Polletta, F., Chen, P., Gardner, B. and Motes, A. (2011) The sociology of storytelling. *The Annual Review of Sociology* 37, 109–130.

Rabinow, P. (ed.) (1991) *The Foucault Reader: An Introduction to Foucault's Thought.* London: Penguin.

Rappler (2016) Filipino Trainee 'Died From Overwork': Japan's Labor Ministry. See https://www.rappler.com/move-ph/balikbayan/149527-filipino-trainee-death-overwork-japan.

Ricoeur, P. (2005) *The Course of Recognition* (D. Pellauer, trans.). Cambridge, MA: Harvard University Press.

Roberts, C. (1997) The politics of transcription. Transcribing talk: Issues of representation. *TESOL Quarterly* 31 (1), 161–171.

Russell, J.G. (2018) Face the reality of racism in Japan. *The Japan Times.* See https://www.japantimes.co.jp/opinion/2018/06/03/commentary/japan-commentary/face-reality-racism-japan/#.XJdf_NHgpPM. Accessed Dec 1, 2019.

Sacks, H. (1974) On the analysability of stories by children. In R. Turner (ed.) *Ethnomethodology: Selected Readings* (pp. 216–232). Harmondsworth: Penguin Books.

Said, S.B. (2015) Teacher identity development in the midst of conflicting ideologies. In Y.L. Cheung, S.B. Said and K. Park (eds) *Advances and Current Trends in Language Teacher Identity Research* (pp. 148–161). London: Routledge.

Sato, M. (2012) Minimum vocabularies needed in Japanese work environment for ALTs. *Akita International Exchange Center Bulletin* 1, 53–63.

Serrano, L.A.S and Schrader, U. (2018) Leadership emergence within MEXTESOL. In A. Elsheikh, C. Coombe and O. Effiong (eds) *The Role of Language Teacher Associations in Professional Development* (pp. 201–214). Basel: Springer.

Simon-Maeda, A. (2005) The complex construction of professional identities: Female EFL educators in Japan speak out. *TESOL Quarterly* 38 (3), 405–436.

Simon-Maeda, A. (2011) *Being and Becoming a Speaker of Japanese: An Autoethnographic Account*. Bristol: Multilingual Matters.

Skutnabb-Kangas, T. and Phillipson, R. (1989) 'Mother tongue': The theoretical and sociopolitical construction of a concept. In U. Ammon (ed.) *Status and Function of Languages and Language Varieties* (pp. 450–477). Boston: De Gruyter.

Song, J. (2016) Emotions and language teacher identity: Conflicts, vulnerability and transformation. *TESOL Quarterly* 50 (3), 631–654.

Spivak, G. (1988) *Can the Subaltern Speak?* Basingstoke: Macmillan.

Stephenson, L. (2018) Developing leadership capacity through leadership learning opportunities. In A. Elsheikh, C. Coombe and O. Effiong (eds) *The Role of Language Teacher Associations in Professional Development* (pp. 187–200). Basel: Springer.

Swales, J. (1990) *Genre Analysis: English in Academic Research Settings*. Cambridge: Cambridge University Press.

Swales, J. (1998) *Other Floors, Other Voices: A Textography of a Small University Building*. Mahwah, NJ: Lawrence Erlbaum.

Swan, A., Aboshiha, P. and Holliday, A. (eds) (2015) *(En)Countering Native-Speakerism: Global Perspectives*. Basingstoke: Palgrave.

Stewart, A. (2005) Teaching positions: A study of identity in English language teachers in Japanese higher education. Unpublished dissertation. Institute of Education, London University.

Stewart, A. (2007) Teacher development and ad hoc communities. *Learning Learning* 14 (1), 18–26.

Stewart, A. and Miyahara, M. (2016) Language teacher associations in Japan: Knowledge producers and/or knowledge disseminators. *ELT Journal* 70 (2), 137–149.

Tajfel, H. and Turner, J.C. (1979) An integrative theory of intergroup conflict. In W.G. Austin and S. Worchel (eds) *The Social Psychology of Intergroup Relations* (pp. 33–53). Monterey, CA: Brooks/Cole.

Tajino, A. and Tajino, Y. (2000) Native and non-native: What can they offer? Lessons from team-teaching in Japan. *ELT Journal* 54 (1), 3–11.

Taylor, C. (1989) *Sources of the Self*. Cambridge: Cambridge University Press.

Taylor, C. (1994) The politics of recognition. In A. Gutmann (ed.) *Multiculturalism and the Politics of Recognition* (pp. 25–75). Princeton, NJ: Princeton University Press.

Tembe, J. and Norton, B. (2008) Promoting local languages in Ugandan primary schools: The community as stakeholder. *Canadian Modern Language Review* 65 (1), 33–60.

The Douglas Fir Group (2015) A transdisciplinary framework for SLA in a multilingual world. *The Modern Language Journal* 100, 19–47.

Tsui, A. (2003) *Understanding Expertise in Teaching: Case Studies of Second Language Teachers*. Cambridge: Cambridge University Press.

Turnbull, B. (2018) Perceptions of value in Japanese English education: Self-reflections of ALTs on the JET programme. *Asian Journal of English Language Teaching* 27, 83–111.

Tyner, J.A. (2004) *Made in the Philippines: Gendered Discourses and the Making of Migrants*. London: Routledge Curzon.

Uludag, P. (2018) Examining the organisational structure of language teacher organisations. In A. Elsheikh, C. Coombe and O. Effiong (eds) *The Role of Language Teacher Associations in Professional Development* (pp. 13–24). Basel: Springer.

Umeda, Y. (2009) Filipina intermarriage in rural Japan: An anthropological approach. Unpublished PhD dissertation. London School of Economics.

Vandrick, S. (1999) ESL and the colonial legacy: A teacher faces her 'missionary kid' past. In G. Haroian-Guerin (ed.) *The Personal Narrative: Writing Ourselves as Teachers and Scholars* (pp. 63–74). Portland, ME: Calendar Islands.

Vandrick, S. (2009) *Interrogating Privilege: Reflections of a Second Language Educator*. Ann Arbor, MI: University of Michigan Press.

Vandrick, S., Hafernik, J.J. and Messerschmitt, D.S. (1994) Outsiders in academe: Women ESL faculty and their students. *Journal of Intensive English Studies* 8, 37–55.

Varghese, M., Morgan, B., Johnston, B. and Johnson, K. (2005) Theorising language teacher identity: Three perspectives and beyond. *Journal of Language, Identity, and Education* 4 (1), 21–44.

Varghese, M., Motha, S., Park, G., Reeves, J. and Trent, J. (2016) Introduction. Special Issue: Language teacher identity in (multi)lingual educational contexts. *TESOL Quarterly* 50 (3), 545–571.

Vilog, R.B. (2013) Layered migrant identities: The case of Filipino *Nikkeijin* workers in Japan. *International Journal of Humanities and Social Science* 3 (13), 128–137.

Weedon, C. (1997) *Feminist Practice and Poststructuralist Theory* (2nd edn). Oxford: Blackwell.

Weedon, C. (2004) *Identity and Culture*. Milton Keynes: Open University Press.

Wenger, E. (1998) *Communities of Practice: Learning, Meaning, and Identity*. Cambridge: Cambridge University Press.

Wenger, E., McDermott, R. and Snyder, W. (2002) *Cultivating Communities of Practice: A Guide to Managing Knowledge*. Cambridge, MA: Harvard Business Review Press.

White, L. (2017) Human capital and its critics: Gary Becker, institutionalism, and anti-neoliberalism. *GMU Working Paper in Economics* 17 (2). Available at https://papers.ssrn.com/sol3/papers.cfm?abstract_id=2905931. Accessed Dec 1, 2019.

Wolff, D. and De Costa, P. (2017) Expanding the language teacher identity landscape: An investigation of the emotions and strategies of a NNEST. *The Modern Language Journal* 101 (Suppl. 1), 76–90.

Yuan, E.R. (2016) The dark side of mentoring on pre-service language teachers' identity formation. *Teaching and Teacher Education* 55, 188–197.

Zemblyas, M. (2003) Emotions and teacher identity: A poststructuralist perspective. *Teachers and Teaching* 9 (3), 213–238.

Index

advocacy 68-69, 95, 115
  transformational, non-
  transformational advocacy 95
agency 15-16, 115
altruism 83, 107
anonymity 24-25
Althusser, L. 13-14, 16, 18
Appleby, R. 3, 100
Assistant Language Teacher (ALT) 1,
  32, 37, 40, 42, 46, 47, 54, 63,
  84, 86-87, 89-90, 115
autonomy 17, 18, 19, 89, 115
awards 50, 57, 71

Barkhuizen, G. 2, 7, 12, 13, 20, 21
Benson, P. 115
bioecological model of development 120
Block, D. 3, 11, 13, 15, 19, 43, 53, 70,
  90, 115, 117, 118
board of education (BoE) 31, 46, 62, 67,
  84, 85, 86-87, 90, 91, 104, 105,
  107, 110
Bourdieu, P. *see social theory* 43, 51,
  54-55
Bruner, J. 22, 23

capital 51-53, 56, 66, 117, 119
  cultural capital 51,
  human capital 53, 55, 71, 90
  social capital 28, 119
capitalism 6, 32, 90, 118
  late capitalism 6, 32
  the new spirit of capitalism 90
career 32, 46, 50, 53, 54, 61, 63, 67, 70,
  73-92, 95, 97, 100, 102, 106,
  107, 113, 118

career history, career narrative,
  career story 3, 7, 20, 21, 30, 50,
  100, 106, 110, 113
  definition of career 89-90
  ELT as a career 88-91
  portfolio career 90
caring 93
certificates 9, 45, 49, 69, 71, 95, 115,
  116
CHOBET, Community and Home-
  Based English Teachers 65, 95,
  116, 120
commitment 27, 83, 88, 90-91, 95, 110,
  120
communicative language teaching
  (CLT) 39, 56, 102
community 8, 11, 27, 35, 51, 55, 89, 91,
  105, 106, 110, 116, 120
  Community of Practice 120
  discourse communities 120
  disciplinary communities 120
  professional discourse communities
  120
  subaltern community 11
  teacher communities 119-121
corporatisation 67
critical realism *see realism*

Darvin, R. and Norton, B. 51-53, 117
De Fina, A. 7, 112, 121
desire 17, 22, 51, 52, 56-58, 87, 93, 114,
  115
  akogare 56
  desire for recognition 17, 58
  desire to communicate meaning 22
  non-coercive arrangements 56

discourse 14, 15, 21, 22, 24, 113, 114, 120
  discourse of neoliberalism 119
  discourse of managers 90
discourses 6, 12, 14-15, 52, 72, 82, 88, 89, 90
discrimination 6, 32, 41, 49, 50, 55, 63, 116, 118, 120
discursive positions, discursive positioning 16
dispatch agencies 37, 54, 61, 67
Duchêne, A. and Heller, M. 5, 32, 53, 72

eikaiwa 1, 3, 38-40, 50, 54, 57, 100, 108, 112, 118, 121
emotion 4, 7, 14-15, 19, 56, 88, 90, 92, 113
  emotion management, emotion work, emotion labour 56
  emotion research 56
English language teachers 3, 5, 6, 13, 56, 66, 89, 90, 95, 113, 114
English language teaching 1, 5, 11, 82, 114
entertainers 34, 35, 66, 95
epistemology 12, 19, 23
erasure 12
essentialism 94
  anti-essentialist 7
  strategic essentialism 16
ethics 25, 56, 58, 92,
  ethical society 18
  ethical turn 19
ethnic identity 32
expertise 90

feminism 15, 16
Filipino communities 55, 91
Filipino English Teacher in Japan (FETJ) xi, 1, 3, 9-11, 20, 24-25, 31-32, 43, 45, 48-49, 59-72, 75, 80, 82-83, 85-88, 91-95, 99, 100, 106, 110-112, 113, 115, 117, 119-120
Filipino identity 3, 6, 11, 65, 86, 109, 112, 119
  stereotypes of Filipinos 34, 53, 82
Filipino migration to Japan 33-36
force of utterances 22-23

Foucault, M. 13, 78, 114, 115
Fraser, N. viii, 12, 17-18, 19, 65-66

gender 3, 6, 11, 12, 15-16, 81-82
globalization 2, 38, 42, 52
  definition of globalization 42
Gray, J. and Morton, T. 15-16, 21, 96, 108
Grint, K. 91

hakengaisha, see Dispatch agencies
Hall, S. 15
Hashimoto, K. 40, 42
Holliday, A. 5, 10, 41, 53
Honneth, A. 2, 12, 17-19, 65, 93, 113, 115, 119, 121
Houghton, S. and Rivers, D. 41, 42, 81

identity, identities
  group identity 59-72
  corporate identity 72
  Filipino identity 3, 11, 28, 65, 86, 109, 112, 119
  hafu, hybrid identity 81
  identities-in-practice/identities-in-discourse 13
  identity formation 59-72
  identity inscriptions 2, 6, 7, 11
  identity politics 2-4, 7, 8, 12, 16, 19-20, 24, 110, 114-117, 122
  intersectionality 11, 12, 43, 118
  language identity 6, 53
    multicompetent speakers 9
    native speaker, nonnative speaker 10, 41, 46, 86, 98, 99, 100, 104, 108, 109, 118
  language teacher identity (LTI) 1, 2, 3, 6, 7, 8, 9-29, 32, 40-42, 51, 55, 56, 72, 73, 81, 92, 114, 117, 121-122
  national identity 11, 27, 81, 100, 107, 108, 110
  professional identity 32, 70, 73, 89, 96, 101, 108, 118
  sexual identity 81
immigration to Japan 33-35
  brides, mail-order brides 34
  entertainers 34
  japayuki 34

nikkeijin 33
  skilled labour 35
inclusive practitioner research 122
internationalisation 36, 39, 40, 41
  kokusaika and *nihonjinron* 41
interpretation 23, 121, 122
  interpretation of narrative 23
intersubjective, intersubjectivity 17, 56,
  115
investment 15, 24, 43-58, 113, 117-118
  investment and motivation 117
  investment as metaphor 24, 117-118
  self-investment 113, 117
Irvine, J. and Gal, S. 12

Japan Association for Language
  Teaching (JALT) 27, 96, 101,
  104, 106, 107
Japan
  immigration policy 33, 35
  education policy 36, 38, 39
  japayuki 34, 113
  labour law, labour dispatch law 37,
  54
  multicultural 36, 65
  nikkeijin 33-34
JET Programme 37, 40, 41, 54
Johnston, B. 7, 70, 73, 88, 92-93

Kamhi-Stein, L. 69, 116
Kubota, R. 39, 41

Labov, W. and Waletsky, J. 22, 110
Lamb, T. 67-68, 70
language ideology 12
  native speakerism 5, 41, 113
  linguicism 5
language teacher associations (LTAs) 7,
  59, 67-71, 113
language teaching 1, 10, 67, 69, 117
  advocacy in language teaching 69
  as a career 73, 88-91, 92
  as a profession 70
legitimacy 57, 95, 113, 114
logos 66, 71-72
Lippi-Green, R. 5
Lorente, B. 11, 53, 70, 82

marginalization 11, 41, 114

membership categorisation analysis,
    see also self-categorisation
    analysis 96, 108, 109
metaphor 15, 24, 42, 43, 51, 52, 54, 55,
    73, 83, 114, 117-119, 121
Ministry of Education, Culture, Sports,
    Science and Technology
    (MEXT) 38, 39, 68
moderate value realism *see realism*
morality 73-94
    moral turn 19, *see ethical turn*
    teachers as moral guides 93-94
Morgan, B. 28, 92, 95, 113, 115
Motha, S. 10, 41
Motha and Lin, 56-57
motivation 56, 92, 116, 117, 120
multiculturalism 65, 117
    multicultural Japan 117

Nagatomo, D. 11, 20, 38
narrative 20-25
    big-story, small-story narrative
      approach 21, 23
    career history 7, 10, 30, 100, 106,
      110, 113
    definition of narrative 22-24
    meaning making of experience 21-22
    narrative research 20-26, 121
    narratives as discursive constructions
      20, 25
    normative and evaluative function of
      narrative 22
    presentation of narrative 24-26, 122
native-speakerism 41, 113
    definition of native-speakerism 41
new work order 90
NNEST movement 116
Noddings, N. 93
non-coercive arrangements, *see desire*
Norton, B. 3, 12, 51-52, 54-55, 58, 117

ontology 12, 19, 21, 23
    ontological security 2
oppression 18, 56
othering 81

passion 63, 77, 92, 95
Pavlenko, A. 20, 25, 108, 121
personal pronoun analysis 109-110

Phan, L.H. 93-94

Philippines, the ix, 1, 9, 11, 32-36, 37, 39, 50, 54, 55, 57, 63, 65, 70, 77, 81, 82, 86, 87, 89, 90, 92, 94, 100, 101, 112, 118, 123-124

    Japanese migration to 33

    overseas workers 34, 70

political economy 1, 19, 42, 115, 117

    capitalism 90, 118

        late capitalism 32

    homo economicus 53, 117

    neoliberalism 70, 117

postmodern paladin 73

post-structuralism 2, 4, 12-19, 22, 56, 113

    discourse, discourses 6, 12, 14, 22, 52, 82, 88, 89, 90, 113, 114, 119

    interpellation 14, 17

    subjectivity 2, 14, 17

    subject positions 14, 15, 16, 17

power 39, 51-52, 54, 56, 87, 114, 115

    empowerment 56, 57, 65, 68, 120

    power/knowledge 68, 114

    powerlessness 56, 57

prejudice 4, 5, 6, 7, 19, 23, 41, 43, 47, 50, 55, 63-64, 77, 100, 106, 113

pride 3, 4-5, 6, 7, 18, 19, 23, 28, 47, 50, 55, 63-64, 71, 77, 81, 91, 100, 107, 113, 116, 118

    pride and profit 6, 52, 72

    pride movements 4, 16

privilege 22, 28, 122,

profession 3, 56, 57, 67, 70, 89, 95, 101

    definition of profession 67-68

    professional associations 67-68, 70, 72

    professional development 1, 7, 12, 47, 56, 68, 70, 91, 112, 115

    professional identity 11, 32, 50, 53, 56, 70, 73, 89, 96, 108, 118

profit 6, 42, 52, 55, 71, 72, 117 *see pride and profit*

promotion 5, 69, 116

    promotion of English 5,

    promotion of Filipinos 70, 116

    self-promotion, 70 *see self-branding, self-marketisation*

race 2, 3, 5, 6, 11, 15, 40, 114

racism, neo-racist 5, 10, 18, 28

rationality 19

realism 21

    moderate value realism 19

    critical realism 19

recognition 2, 4-6, 16-20, 55-58, 71-72, 95, 113, 119

    recognition theory 2, 4-6, 16- 20, 28, 93, 113-115

    intersubjective recognition, mutual recognition 115, 119-121

    misrecognition 4, 12-16, 55-56, 113, 121

    struggle for recognition 2, 66

researcher reflexivity 121

Ricoeur, P. 2, 4

rights 2, 5, 16, 17, 18, 28, 41, 53, 69, 108, 121

Sacks, H. 22, 110

self 13, 15, 17-18, 53

    knowledge of self 17

    self-branding 53, 90

    self-categorization analysis 108-109

    self-definition 70, 108

    self-entrepreneur 90

    self-interest 7, 53, 117

    self-investment 113

    self-marketisation 71

    self-naming 8, 11

    self-positioning 107

    self-representation 113

    self-recognition 17-18

social activism 7, 12, 59, 65, 116, 117

social capital 28, 119

social class 3, 6, 11, 12, 19, 112, 114

social identity 11

    social identity categories 108

    social identity theory 22, 108

social justice 3, 18, 19, 65, 66, 69, 113, 115, 119

social status 50, 54, 55, 73, 91, 114, 119

social spheres 91, 92, 121

social theory

    Bourdieu's social theory 43, 51, 55, 117

    capital 51-53, 55, 56, 117, 119

    habitus 51, 54, 55, 56, 117

Honneth's social theory 18, 19, 93, 121
sociolinguistics 5, 12
   accent 5
Spivak, G. 16
stereotypes 34, 39, 53, 82, 106
structure 64, 67, 69, 72, 94, 115
   structure and agency 115
   structure of recognition 17
subaltern 11, 16, 111

Taylor, C. 2, 18, 55-56, 115
teacher education 10, 12, 13, 115, 117, 121

The Douglas Fir Group 12, 120, 121
transdisciplinary 12, 120
transcription 21, 24, 122
transformative, non-transformative advocacy *see advocacy*
transnational person 112

Vandrick, S. 11, 25, 41, 122

Weedon, C. 13-15, 17
work 73-95
   market, social and moral spheres of work 91-91
   new work order 90

For Product Safety Concerns and Information please contact our EU Authorised Representative:

Easy Access System Europe

Mustamäe tee 50

10621 Tallinn

Estonia

gpsr.requests@easproject.com